PRAISE FOR *USEFUL WISDOM*

"Anthony Robinson is many things: pastor, theologian, consultant, preacher, leader, teacher, and more. In this excellent volume, Robinson adds the role of mentor to pastors younger and older. His net of discernment gathers 'useful wisdom' from his long experience in the church, addressing issues in ministry such as public prayer and handling the inevitability of bullies. . . . Robinson provides gentle, wise, and honest guidance."

—Thomas G. Long
Bandy Professor Emeritus of Preaching, Candler School of Theology, Emory University

"Into this lovely, affectionate book, pastor and master church coach Tony Robinson pours a lifetime of insights on the joys and the challenges of pastoral ministry. Tony's steadfast but also critical and experienced love for the vocation of church leadership shines through on every page. Offered as testimony to his daughter who is beginning ministry, Tony gives Paul-to-Timothy guidance that will be strong, realistic, faithful encouragement to anyone in ministry today."

—Will Willimon
Professor of Christian Ministry, Duke Divinity School

"On many a hiking trail, I have been the lucky recipient of my dad's wisdom. Now I'm so glad for myself (and others) to have access to his wisdom, even when retirement hobbies take him out of cell phone range. These letters are a breath of fresh air, a gentle reminder to get back to basics, and a saving grace whenever ministry feels overwhelming or isolating. And I have no doubt they will be this for all who encounter them."

—Laura Robinson
pastor, Bethel United Church of Christ

"This is a generous book filled with seasoned observations and practical counsel. But even more, it is a testament to Tony Robinson's conviction that the pastoral life is a worthy one. His letters brim with encouragement to all who have taken it up, providing much-needed companionship as well as useful wisdom. I am no 'young minister,' but I came away edified, instructed, and grateful."

    —MARY LUTI
    United Church of Christ pastor

"*Useful Wisdom* reminds us of the importance of building relationships across generations and creating safe spaces to share our most vulnerable selves. 'Generational differences are real, but aren't the whole story.' The story of the church is ever unfolding, but it's an incredible gift to receive bread for our journey. *Useful Wisdom* is the manna my soul needed."

    —BRITTANY JULIETTE HANLIN
    Associate Minister, Marble Collegiate Church, New York

"This book brought me back to a time of life I vividly remember: the daily swing, as a new minister, between 'I love this job!' and 'How in the world do I *survive* this job?' Tony Robinson is the wise companion I needed then and still do: someone to help me reflect on my ministry with perspective and purpose. The letters he writes in this book will feel as if they were addressed to you, personally. Read them, and then read them again. In any season of life, this is a book to treasure."

    —ANNA CARTER FLORENCE
    Peter Marshall Professor of Preaching, Columbia Theological Seminary

Useful Wisdom

Useful Wisdom

Letters to Young (and Not-So-Young) Ministers

ANTHONY B. ROBINSON

CASCADE *Books* • Eugene, Oregon

USEFUL WISDOM
Letters to Young (and Not-So-Young) Ministers

Copyright © 2020 Anthony B. Robinson. All rights reserved. Except for brief quotations in critical publications or reviews, no part of this book may be reproduced in any manner without prior written permission from the publisher. Write: Permissions, Wipf and Stock Publishers, 199 W. 8th Ave., Suite 3, Eugene, OR 97401.

Quotations from the Bible are from The New Revised Standard Version (NRSV), unless specifically noted otherwise. New Revised Standard Version Bible, copyright 1989, Division of Christian Education of the National Council of the Churches of Christ in the United States.

Cascade Books
An Imprint of Wipf and Stock Publishers
199 W. 8th Ave., Suite 3
Eugene, OR 97401

www.wipfandstock.com

PAPERBACK ISBN: 978-1-5326-8343-5
HARDCOVER ISBN: 978-1-5326-8344-2
EBOOK ISBN: 978-1-5326-8345-9

Cataloguing-in-Publication data:

Names: Robinson, Anthony B.

Title: Useful wisdom: letters to young (and not-so-young) ministers / Anthony B. Robinson.

Description: Eugene, OR: Cascade Books, 2020 | Includes bibliographical references.

Identifiers: ISBN 978-1-5326-8343-5 (paperback) | ISBN 978-1-5326-8344-2 (hardcover) | ISBN 978-1-5326-8345-9 (ebook)

Subjects: LCSH: Pastoral theology.

Classification: BV4011 .R55 2020 (paperback) | BV4011 (ebook)

Manufactured in the U.S.A.   03/18/20

Dedicated to
Brittany Juliette Hanlin and Laura Kanoelani Rose Robinson
and the church of the future

Contents

Introduction | xi

PART ONE: SOME BASICS

   A Sense of Purpose | 3
   By the Way, What Is the Gospel? | 7
   The Marks of the Church | 10

PART TWO: HOW DO I LIVE WITH THIS JOB?

   What Keeps Me Grounded? | 17
   Self-Care | 22
   Boundaries | 25
   Remaining Faithful Amid Trials | 29

PART THREE: SHOP CRAFT

   Starting Out in a New Call | 35
   Praying in Public | 39
   Relationships with Colleagues | 43
   Meetings, Meetings, Meetings | 47
   Inviting God to the Meeting | 50
   Is There a Word from the Lord? | 53
   Leadership | 57
   Prophetic Leadership | 61
   How Long Should I Stay? | 65

PART FOUR: TOUGH STUFF

    Personnel Issues | 71
    Bullies | 74
    The Former Pastor Problem | 77
    Money | 81

PART FIVE: THE FUTURE OF THE CHURCH

    Dealing with the Narrative of Decline | 87
    How Do We Breathe Life into the Institutional Church? | 91

PART SIX: THE CHURCH OF THE FUTURE

    Building the Front Porch | 97
    Telling the Truth | 101
    Pay Attention to the Energy | 106
    Rethinking "Mission" | 111

Conclusion | 114

Bibliography | 117

Introduction

Two of my favorite young ministers were colleagues at Plymouth Church, United Church of Christ in Des Moines, Iowa, when they contacted me with the following request.

"Would you," they asked, "write us some letters with your advice about a bunch of things we are trying to figure out? We'll provide the list of questions and topics."

As it happens, one of these two is my daughter, Laura Robinson. The other is her friend and colleague, Brittany Hanlin.*

I was flattered by their request and by their confidence. Brittany and Laura, in coming up with their idea, were swimming against the stream. The prevailing wisdom these days holds that the different generations don't have much to say to one another. Each is so unique they have a different name. Moreover, the gap between my "boomer" generation and their "millennial" one is alleged to be especially vast.

Their request harkens to an earlier, and I think wiser, time. One in which wisdom was passed, lovingly, from generation to generation. Generational differences are real, but aren't the whole story. The notion that there is nothing to be passed on, that one's generation and experience are so unique that others have nothing to give to us or say to us, is, well, historically unprecedented and foolish.

There is wisdom to be shared from one generation to another. When offering such counsel, caution and humility are always a good idea. But sharing what we've learned is also a good thing.

xi

Introduction

This is one of my hopes and intentions in offering this collection of epistles. With humility, I want to share what I've learned and am learning. Thank you, Brittany and Laura, for asking.

Here's another hope I have for this little collection. I want Brittany and Laura, and really all clergy, not only to survive in ministry, but more—to thrive in ministry. While there are days when surviving may seem the very best we can hope for, it isn't, not really. We should hope to thrive in a vocation that is in service to the One who came to bring life and "bring it abundantly."

That's my second hope for this collection, that ministers of the church who read it might find encouragement and insights for thriving in this work.

Here's a third hope I harbor for these epistles—that reading each might help you who read them to get a little distance or perspective as you live into your calling. Ron Heifetz, who teaches leadership at Harvard's Kennedy School, introduced many to an idea he called, "Getting to the balcony." (I think Jesus was onto to something similar, well before Heifetz, when he stole away from his public ministry for times of prayer.)

What Heifetz means by "getting to the balcony" is that all who serve as leaders need to regularly step back, or up above the metaphorical dance floor of congregational life, to get a better look at the complex situation in which they are working and trying to lead.

Think of a congregation as the swirling crowd on a dance floor. At floor level and in the midst of the action, it is difficult to see what is going on, to get the big picture and see how the parts and whole are related.

So, "get to the balcony," up above the swirling dance floor to see more clearly. From there you may notice who's dancing with whom, as well as who's dancing and who's not. You may see how close to the music some are, as well as those who keep their distance. From above, you may detect patterns and relationships.

To be able to have such a perspective, a bit of distance, is an essential skill for clergy both to survive and to thrive. My hope is that when you sit down to read one of these letters it will provide you with a chance to step back, to gain perspective, and to take a fresh look. I hope to take you to the balcony.

INTRODUCTION

So, I offer what I have learned in forty years of ministry in a variety of congregations and settings—congregations urban and rural, small and large, most primarily Caucasian but some multiracial and multicultural. My experience also includes teaching in seminaries, speaking at clergy conferences, teaching preaching, coaching clergy, and serving as a consultant to congregations in a wide variety of settings and denominations.

I believe in the church and in the ministry. I also know it can be—will be—when done well and conscientiously, tough work. I hope these letters provide encouragement, a few good ideas, and companionship in this hard, good work.

Sending love, your friend in Christ and companion in ministry.

*Both have now concluded their two years in the Lilly Endowment founded "Transitions-Into-Ministry" program at Plymouth in Des Moines. At present, Brittany is an Associate Minister at Marble Collegiate Church in New York City. Laura is the Minister at Bethel United Church of Christ, in White Salmon, Washington.

PART ONE

Some Basics

A Sense of Purpose

DEAR ONES,

Thank you so much for the invitation to write these letters to you. And thank you for the list of suggested topics. It is a great list. It did strike me as heavy on—what should I call it?—"how in the world do you live with this job?" I get that. Two colleagues of mine titled their book about pastoral ministry, *This Odd and Wondrous Calling*.[1] It really is both, odd and wondrous. And it is one that can overwhelm us with its multiple and relentless demands.

During my own first pastorate, I remember feeling "I love this job" (at least most of the time). I really did. I felt engaged, challenged, and alive as I did it. But at the very same time, I wondered, "How in the world do you live with this job?" That is, how do you keep things (including yourself) in perspective? How to do prioritize other important commitments and relationships, like family and friends? How do you keep from being overwhelmed by work that doesn't ever get finished?

Such questions lurk in many of the topics you have suggested. And I will address those topics: self-care, prayer, church politics, boundaries, relationships with colleagues, directly in subsequent letters.

But I want to begin this series of letters by coming at these questions from another angle and, at least for now, indirectly. People have often asked me over the years, "How do you stay fresh?

---

1. Copenhaver and Daniel, *This Odd and Wondrous Calling*.

Part One: Some Basics

Engaged? Alive?" "How do you keep going?" "What renews you?" "How do you keep from burning out?"

Well, the short answer is that I haven't always managed to avoid something like burnout. There have been times when I was overwhelmed, depressed, filled with doubt, and not entirely sure I could make it through another week or another board meeting or another stewardship campaign (Lord, have mercy!).

I think we have to expect that such times and seasons are a part of life and ministry and accept that. There are seasons of great joy and fruitfulness. And there are seasons of discouragement when we wonder if anything we are doing matters. Often in the midst of it, the tough times loom larger and seem longer than they are. When you look back they seem to diminish. Looking back, the joy, like the cream on milk in the old milk bottle days, rises.

That said, I feel that I have kept going, "kept the faith" as Paul puts it, and really loved the ministry over these many years. And the thing that has been most important for me in managing that—and my answer when people ask—"What keeps you alive? What keeps you going?"—is that I believe in what I am doing.

One needs a sense of purpose.

With a strong sense of purpose, you can face a lot. Without a sense of purpose, the whole thing unravels or becomes something you are doing so that you have a pension. Neither is a good way to go.

So, a sense of purpose. A sense of purpose is what gets you out of bed in the morning. It is what sustains you when you find yourself thinking, "Sunday—again, already, really?"

Purpose—why are you doing what you are doing? What's the point? The intention? The goal?

Here's a bit of an aside, though it is actually pretty central. I have come to the conclusion that often the issues we clergy wrestle with are also the same issues that our congregations wrestle with as a community. That is to say, a congregation also faces the question of purpose.

Peter Drucker, a famous business consultant and a committed Episcopal layperson, typically asked his clients two questions. They become known as "The Drucker questions." What business are you in?

A Sense of Purpose

How's business?

Business, for my purposes and in this context, can be considered another word for *purpose*. Asking "what business you are in?" is a way of asking, "What's your purpose? What are you trying to do, or to accomplish?"

My observation is that congregations that have a fairly clear and strong sense of purpose—what the French call *raison d'etre* (reason for being)—tend to thrive. Conversely, congregations that aren't giving much thought or prayer to why they are here, or lack a compelling *raison d'etre*, tend to be in decline. As leaders, one of our jobs is to help congregations stay "on purpose." More on that later.

But this is also true for clergy. If your sense of purpose is strong and reasonably clear, it will keep you going. If you lack a clear and strong sense of purpose, devote some quality time to the subject. If that doesn't work, consider another line of work.

So, let me wrap this letter up by sharing what animates me as a minister, that is, my sense of purpose.

Most basic, I trust in the God revealed in creation, exodus, crucifixion—resurrection. I believe in the power of this God to transform the lives of individuals and communities. I trust in the grace of this God, by which I mean the way God finds us when we are lost, heals us when we are broken, and raises us up when we are as good as dead. As a pastor and preacher, I get to tell the story of this God.

Closely related, I love the Bible, the Scriptures of the church. I could say "I believe in the Bible" but "love" is better because this really is a relationship. The Scriptures have an amazing power. When we listen to them, God speaks to us through them in a way that changes things. As a preacher and a teacher I get to be in regular conversation with Scripture and to invite others into the conversation.

A third part of my sense of purpose extends beyond a basic trust and faith in God and God's grace and a love of the Scriptures, to include the Christian faith as a rich and living tradition of thought and practice, one that extends over thousands of years and many cultures. We steward "saving truths." This faith is, one might say, a lens through which we construe life in a particular way,

Part One: Some Basics

a cross-shaped way. As a preacher, teacher, and writer I have loved championing the dialogue between the riches of this faith tradition and the issues and challenges of human life.

And I believe in the church. The church is a frail vessel that frequently disappoints, but just as often astonishes with its beauty and grace. I tend to think of the church as a school, although different than a formal classroom-type school. In the church, we teach and embody a way of life, a way of life following Jesus Christ. The church is full of the most wildly human people, endlessly fascinating in their own right. But here's the kicker: often in unexpected ways, God manages to work through this ornery, wonderful, confused, and courageous people. Working among these people, this community, as a leader, pastor, and teacher is a great privilege.

As an ordained minister, I get to be an instrument, often a frail and imperfect one, but an instrument nonetheless, of this God and God's grace at work in the world.

You will describe your sense of purpose in your own words. Nor should you measure your words against mine. Mine would not have been so fully formed when I was your age.

Still, my point is that a fairly strong, reasonably clear sense of purpose is at the heart of staying alive and engaged amid the very real challenges and frustrations of this strange and wondrous calling.

Sending love . . .

By the Way, What Is the Gospel?

Dear Ones,

 A longtime friend of mine, a journalist, has a habit of innocently asking the most disarming basic questions. Often these are questions about something that there seems to be an assumption "everyone" knows what you're talking about. So, if you ask, you must be a knucklehead. So you don't ask. After all, who wants to be thought a knucklehead? The problem is that the basic questions go begging in the silence.

 In a seminary class or church, people may use the words "the gospel," or to up the ante a bit, "the gospel of Jesus Christ." Have you ever thought, I wonder what that really means? But since everyone else seems to know, no one asks the obvious question. My journalist friend uses his outside observer status to ask the "dumb" questions.

 Which sometimes turn out to be the very best questions.

 "What is the gospel?" might be one of those.

 Okay, so "gospel" means "good news." But what is "the good news"?

 I bring this up because while people may refer to "the gospel" I often think that what I hear (and sometimes what I say) in church sounds a lot more like good advice than good news. We encourage people to do this, think that, or feel this way or that. The focus is on us. And there's a heavy hit of "should."

 Here's the first thing about "the gospel." It's not about you (or me). It is about God. The gospel is the news about who God is and what God has done, what God is doing and what God has promised. And it turns out that this God acts in ways that we humans mostly don't expect, often don't like, and frequently find surprising.

Part One: Some Basics

There's a simple way to assess whether a sermon is a message of the gospel. Look at the subject of the verbs. If we humans are the subject of all or most of the verbs, as in "we think," or "we should think," or "we ought," or "we have done this or that," chances are that it isn't good news. It may be good advice or boasting or guilt tripping, but if we humans are the subject of all the verbs it isn't gospel. If it's the gospel, God is at least sometimes the subject of the verbs. Words like, "God loves," "God opens a way," "God changes lives," "God does unexpected things with people we never imagined were on God's radar."

In order to talk this way, you need to believe first, that there is a God, and second, that this God is active and up to something in the world. The Bible is a story that tries to initiate us into this way of thinking and seeing life. But there's a strong counterforce, I'll call it "modernity" for short. "Modernity" boils everything down to rational explanations and only counts stuff like data or facts. Which is fine as far as it goes. Only it doesn't go far enough.

The theologian, William Placher, in a book called *Unapologetic Theology*, has a little riff that I have found enormously helpful in this regard. He writes, "As I read the biblical stories and as I use them to try to understand my own life, I also come to realize that in these stories God's initiative has a kind of priority.

"Abraham does not think he has just taken a notion to travel; he thinks he is responding to God's call. Samuel does not just choose David; he anoints David as God's choice. Jeremiah calls the people back to faithfulness to a God who has never abandoned them. I find myself wanting to say similar things about my own life as a Christian: my acts of love seem a response, however inadequate, to a love that loved me first; my projects, when they are for good, make sense to me as parts of a larger plan."[2]

The key here is God's initiative, an active God who is creating, calling, seeking, finding, disrupting, and forgiving.

In language that is somewhat more blunt, the Lutheran preacher Nadia Bolz Weber writes, "I'm not running after Jesus, Jesus is running my ass down."[3] God's initiative.

---

2. Placher, *Unapologetic Theology*, 133–34.
3. Bolz-Weber, *Accidental Saints*, 29.

By the Way, What Is the Gospel?

One of the problems in churches that have drunk heavily at the wells of modernity is a loss of confidence in God's initiative, in a God who acts. When you lose that confidence you are apt to talk mostly about human action, i.e., what you should think, feel, or do. Incidentally, when people say "don't preach to me," they are mostly meaning that kind of finger-wagging talk. No good news in it. While exhortation has a place, if it gets too far from grace and the news of God, it doesn't wear well.

For most Christians "the gospel" focuses on what God has done and is doing in Jesus. So, they may speak of Jesus who has torn down dividing walls between groups (Ephesians), or died for the ungodly (Romans), or rose from death so that death might have no power over us (1 Corinthians).

Note that all of these ways of speaking gospel are about God's activity and initiative. God makes the first move. And God gets the last word.

Another way to put this is to say that the thing that makes Christianity different from other religions or life philosophies is grace. Grace is God's doing, God's initiative. It is running our ass down when we may be (like Jonah) running away from life, love, and God.

Often people think that Christianity is about all the things you and I must or should do to get on God's good side or to show others that we're on God's side.

Nope. In fact, when we are frantically trying to do all the stuff that shows how great we are and that we're on God's side, God will often say, "STOP IT, RIGHT NOW." (Experientially that may feel like hitting a wall.)

Because the gospel isn't about all the stuff we should be doing to show everyone that we are on God's side. The gospel is, "In Jesus Christ I have taken your side and will never leave it. Trust this and LIVE."

Our lives, as Bill Placher put it, are a response to a love that loved us first. That's the gospel.

Sending love . . .

The Marks of the Church

Dear Ones,

One of the challenges I have experienced as a minister and congregational leader was knowing where to place priority and energy—my own and that of the church. Another way to put this is that churches have a tendency to spread themselves thin. Someone said, "Lots of churches suffer from the Pecos River syndrome—they are a mile wide but only a foot deep."

Also, there's something called the 80/20 principal. Eighty percent of our efforts yield twenty percent of the results, while twenty percent result in eighty. Without being efficiency freaks, how do we spend more of our time and energy doing the things that really matter? What are the "vital few,"[4] things that we, as a church and you as a minister, need to do and do well in order to faithful and fruitful?

I'm talking about setting priorities. As a minister, you really have quite a bit of freedom. Given that, you need to set priorities. But how? On what basis? Is it the old "squeaky wheel gets the grease"? Moreover, leaders help congregations to set priorities. But how?

One useful guide is what some refer to as "the four marks of the church." Often what people mean when they use that term are the

---

4. "The vital few" is a concept I picked up from the business world. The idea is that there are a few things that are absolutely vital to success in our business, whatever that may be. Figure out what those are and do them well. For churches, this can be adapted to ask, "What are the vital few things we need to do and do well to be faithful and fruitful?"

The Marks of the Church

"marks" drawn from the Nicene Creed. There the church is confessed as, "one," "holy," "catholic" (meaning universal), and "apostolic."

That's great, but another, and to my mind, more useful set of marks of the church can be drawn from the story of the earliest church in the Acts of the Apostles. In the book of Acts there are several capsule summaries of the life of the church, like Acts 2:43–46 and Acts 4:32–34. Here we find four "marks" that have seemed to me a useful guide to what the life of the church involves.

We'll unpack them shortly, but here they are in the Greek: *kerygma, didache, koinonia,* and *diakonia*. No translation quite catches everything in those words, but it is fair to sum these up as proclamation and celebration of the good news/worship (*kerygma*); teaching the faith/education and faith formation (*didache*); being a community/fellowship (*koinonia*); and service to those in need (*diakonia*).

If you're covering those bases, what's happening is "church," which isn't so much a building or an organization as an event and a living system or, in Paul's metaphor, a body.

Okay, so here's more on each of the four.

Generally speaking, worship is the central event in the life of a church, and it should be. It may be the one thing we do, as church, that is unique to us. A focus on the *kerygma* means are we hearing the word of God and the good news of the gospel proclaimed, and we are experiencing it embodied in our celebration of the sacraments. I see worship as the beating heart of the church, the powerful organ from which life flows to all parts of the body. If worship is tepid, boring, or indifferent the body is likely to be weak, maybe ill. Worship, the experience of being in God's presence together, can be transformative, restoring perspective, and moving people to faith. A minister friend says that her operative assumption is that most of the people who show up for worship have, in a week of challenge and struggle, "lost" their faith. We come to have faith renewed. We come week by week to be evangelized, that is to be dumbstruck all over again by the good news. Worship deserves our best effort and energies.

Didache was the word of the early church for teaching. Teaching is a little different than preaching, although the line between the two can be fuzzy. Good sermons do teach. But the church's teaching is generally a step back to say, what do we mean? What's the background and context?

Teaching tends to be either informational or formational. Information is stuff about a topic. Formation is about becoming a particular kind of person. There's plenty of room for both in the life of the church, but in the end, we are more in the formation, the people-making business, than the information business. We are trying to be and to form particular kinds of people, followers of Jesus. To do that we sometimes teach in classrooms or other school-like settings. But equally often, teaching happens in other settings. Like serving those in need, or being present at the time of crisis or loss, or working through a tough issue or conflict. Jesus did some teaching in the synagogue (a kind of classroom), but most of his teaching happened in the midst of life, drawing on what was going on in front of him.

Koinonia is the Greek word for fellowship or community. This ranges from what some have called the true sacrament of the Protestant church, the "coffee hour," to small group gatherings, to having a supper or a party together. As with *didache*, there's an overlap here with worship. Nothing creates a stronger sense of our life together, of being a community of true fellowship, than powerful worship. But *koinonia* is more. It is shared life.

Diakonia means service, service to those in need. In Acts the early church famously shared "everything," taking care to provide for the needs of everyone in the community and especially the "widows and orphans," which is way of saying, "the most vulnerable among us." Again, this takes all sorts of forms from a soup kitchen, to visiting people in prison, to working to provide shelter and home for those who have none, to speaking out against injustice.

In Acts, this service tended to focus on people who were part of the Christian community. The idea there seemed to be that the life of this community—where the needy were included and no one went without—would be a sign to the wider world of a different way of being.

You can use these four marks from the book of Acts as a kind of template to think about and assess the life of a congregation.

Where are we strong? What needs work? Are we missing something? How do the four fit together and interact?

Moreover, you can think of the church, using these four marks, as a story-formed, story-embodying people. In worship we tell, sing, celebrate, and proclaim the story of what God has done and is doing. In teaching we learn the story, the Christian and biblical story. We consider how these stories interact with the stories being told in our world. Life in community means being the story, while service is our attempt to do the story. We are stewards of a particular story about a loving, faithful, gracious, and surprising God. Our job, you might say, is to tell, teach, be and do this sacred story and in doing so to form a people who are "a light to the world, and salt to the earth."

Sending love . . .

PART TWO

How Do I Live with This Job?

What Keeps Me Grounded?

DEAR ONES,
 The idea of being grounded comes from electronics. A "grounding wire" keeps the system or appliance connected to the earth, which it turns out is really important. When the system or a part of it gets overloaded or too hot, the earth acts as a reservoir to absorb the charge and keep it from blowing out all the circuits.
 There are times that we too get overloaded (churches do too). Too much stuff coming at you is a hazard of the ministry. And sometimes we just get overheated. So how do we stay grounded, connected with the earth, both literally and metaphorically?
 Here are ten things that keep me grounded. Some might be considered "spiritual practices." Others are probably best described as "life practices."

"Grace"

Often these days when we speak of "spiritual practices" the emphasis falls on what we do or should do (chanting, breathing, cleansing, journaling, drumming, meditating, centering—really, it can be overwhelming). For me what God has done and is doing is more important and powerful. Before our search for God comes God's search for us. Experientially for me, that means that grace—new beginnings and a renewal of energy—happen. As a gift. I cannot fully explain and still less can I control this, but it is real.

Or to put it another way, God is God and I am not. Thank God. That keeps me grounded.

"Scripture"

I love the Bible. This is a learned affection, born of study, struggle, and listening. The Bible is not as easy book nor one whose meaning is self-evident. But if you can shut up and/or ask some good questions, it will speak. Or better, God will speak through it. The Scriptures aren't old and dead, they are alive.

I love savoring the Bible's internal dialogue, tensions, and seeming contradictions. The Scripture is one of the primary ways I experience God's active grace, the way its texts and stories speak and create a new reality.

"The Three N's"

A psychiatric nurse with whom I worked on a hospital staff introduced me to this. It is one of the best "prescriptions" I know for dealing with stress or situational depression.

The first "N" stands for "nurturing." Do something that nurtures you. Often for me that is being in nature (the woods, a beach), listening to music, or reading poetry. Taking a nap also counts. Writing out some personal affirmations can be good. That may sound a little hokey, writing personal affirmations, like "I am a good friend," or "I am a good preacher who takes my work seriously," but sometimes the negative voices in our heads can get up a real head of steam. An intervention is needed. Changing the internal dialogue helps.

The second "N" is new. Do something that is "new" to you. It doesn't have to be a huge thing. It could be walking on the grass barefoot when it is dewy in the morning (if you've never done that before), or going a park or library or part of town where you've not been before. Or extend grace to yourself. That might be new. You extend it to others—how about to yourself? Go to the symphony if you're never been, or to a nightclub to hear a musician you've never heard of. You get the idea.

And the third "N" is "No." Politely decline a request, a proposal, an appointment, an invitation, or a task that doesn't have your name on it or just isn't something that you need to do. Sometimes when we're in a low space we say "yes" to too much or to things that aren't really us. Saying "no" can be a fine act of self-care.

So, the three N's: nurturing, new, and no. Do one a day. Overdosing—doing two N's or even all three—is also okay.

"Gratitude List"

I sit down most evenings and write out a list of at least ten things that I am grateful for that day. Some things repeat, like "health" and "family." Others are unique to that day, "time spent with X," "a beautiful sunset."

I might not have managed this as a daily practice when we had small children and work was full-time, but even if you don't do it daily, doing a gratitude list is a good thing to do whenever you are feeling low or feel like life has done you wrong. I generally do my gratitude list toward the end of the day, so it is a sort of written down prayer of thanksgiving.

"Solvitur Ambulando"

This is Latin which translates, more or less, to "It is solved by walking." When blocked on writing a sermon or tied in knots about a parish problem, a walk is a good idea. Ambulate. Get the body moving. And often, that gets you out in the natural world, which is in itself grounding.

"Give It Five Minutes"

This is a variation on "counting to ten backwards" or other things to do when it's probably best not say anything for a few minutes lest you say something you will seriously regret.

Part Two: How Do I Live with This Job?

When you feel like you want to tear someone's head off or launch into a bitter soliloquy of self-justification, "Give it five minutes." And during that time *solvitur ambulando*.

"Morning Prayer"

I do not regard myself as a model for a prayer life. But this is what I do. I am a morning person, which means that I am usually up before anyone else. I get to my knees, a posture I trust. I say the Lord's Prayer. Then I pray for others, then for myself. I end with the Serenity Prayer: "God, grant me the serenity to accept the things I cannot change, the courage to change the things I can, and the wisdom to know the difference." Then I get up and have a cup of coffee.

What to pray about? Usually it is the stuff you are most sad about, mad about, or glad about. Urgency, I suspect, counts more with God than eloquence.

"Reading"

For me reading, at least some reading, is pretty close to, maybe even a form of prayer. It is a way of nurturing my inner life and of listening for God. Really good writing, fiction or non-fiction, is something that prompts me to further reflection. It slows me down. It grounds me. As does,

"Writing"

To me the written word is magic. By writing, I sort out what I think. Often in writing things for this or that, I start with a half-baked idea and find that, as I write, it cooks and becomes something almost edible.

I don't keep a journal exactly, but I am writing something—a sermon, an article, a blog, a talk, or just my musings—most days. This may not be your thing (none of the above may be your thing), but the point is to find those practices that are yours and make them part of your life.

"Pay Attention to Your ADL's"

Activities of Daily Life (ADL's) are not to be minimized. Eating, sleeping, personal hygiene, exercise. Many of us tend to eat on the roller coaster model: nothing for a long time, then too much and the wrong stuff. Better to eat smaller amounts more frequently. Always keep a protein bar (I like the "Pure Protein" bars) in your purse or desk. It is not a good idea to do hard meetings or pastoral visits when your blood sugar is way low.

Sleep and exercise are also amazing. When personal hygiene starts to slip, that's a blinking red light. It concerns me that many clergy are terribly overweight. Of course, the whole population is overweight. But carrying around an extra twenty-five pounds eats up your energy and probably doesn't do a lot for self-esteem. Staying in decent shape is important for our functioning, and also because, like it or not, how we live does influence others.

Sending love . . .

Self-Care

Dear Ones,

"Self-care" is not a term that I recall hearing when I was your age. It seems to have come into common usage in the last twenty-five years or so, both in the world of the church and in the wider world.

If I don't recall hearing the terms "self-care" early in my ministry, I do recall hearing a lot of young clergy—including myself—going on at considerable length about just how busy we were. When I would get together with colleagues, it was as if we were having a "I'm busier than you" pissing contest.

I'm sure I played that game with the best of them, but after a while I dropped out. I did that because I sensed beneath our lament a note of false pride. "I'm so needed! I'm needed so much that I am busy all the time. Did I mention how much I am needed?" (Note to the careful reader: this suggests that at least sometimes we are unindicted co-conspirators in our own extreme busyness.)

Beyond that, it occurred to me that if I was too busy or too tired or too whatever, dealing with that was really on me. Complaining to others might let off some steam, but it didn't change anything. God knows, the church wasn't going to deal with it. The denomination or the conference minister might point to relevant resources or a workshop here or there, but they weren't going to fix this one. Nor would one's Pastoral Relations Committee, which was in some vague way charged with "caring for the pastor," going to solve it.

It was up to me.

It was up to me to set my priorities, manage my schedule, to learn to say "no," and to take care of myself.

Self-Care

Still, when the term "self-care" did eventually find its way into our vocabulary, my first reaction was, I confess, to pooh-pooh it. Hearing the words "self-care" I somehow heard "weakness" or "self-indulgence."

In that judgment, I was wrong.

I have come to believe that genuine self-care isn't weak or self-indulgent. Rather, it is both essential and demanding.

Good self-care is difficult for a host of reasons that bear some reflection. One is the Christian faith. To be a Christian, many of us have thought and been taught, is to lead a life that is self-sacrificial. There's a whole lot in the Bible that appears to tell us exactly that. Jesus says we must "lose ourselves" if we want to "find ourselves." He speaks of being "servants" of all. And Paul reminds us that, "It is always more blessed to give than to receive."

I am not sure a common understanding of these passages—as a call to always put the interests and needs of others ahead of our own—is correct. What's more, if you look for them, you will find other texts and perspectives. Jesus frequently retreated, disappeared really, to be alone. He did say "no," at least sometimes, when people asked things of him. And Paul also wrote, "Each one must carry their own load."

I am not sure this matter can be solved or resolved by debating biblical texts and admonitions.

What I am sure about is that if you always put other people's needs ahead of your own, there's a good chance you will end up being full of anger and resentment, and of little good to anyone, least of all yourself. You will be too frazzled, too irritable, too empty.

Or worse.

What could be worse? Worse is when you deny your own self and needs so relentlessly that they find some distorted way to come out (you can bet they will), a way that does damage not just to you but to other people. You become mean. You are dishonest with yourself and those you care most about. You tip into substance abuse or have an affair with a parishioner. None of those things will turn out well.

Self-care is also difficult and important because real self-care not only means prioritizing the basics—good rest, good food, good

Part Two: How Do I Live with This Job?

exercise, and those experiences that make us laugh and give us joy—it means coming to grips with your own stuff. We have all got stuff. Each and every one of bears wounds that if we don't get at least some grip on, will take the upper hand in our lives.

So, good self-care does include the above-mentioned basics (without apology or guilt), and it probably also includes a good therapist or spiritual director and friends who can speak truth to us. We are pretty good at deceiving ourselves.

We need wise others, people who care about us but aren't wrapped up in the same dramas we are, to help us gain perspective and see the part we are playing in the mess in which we find ourselves. Ultimately, these wise others or confidants don't have the answers for us. We have the answers, or we plus God have the answers. But these people can listen to us. We all, and perhaps especially clergy—who if they are good at their work do lots of listening—need people who listen well to them.

In the end, I think practicing good self-care means recognizing that God is God and we are not. Clergy are particularly susceptible to playing God or imagining that we possess God-like attributes of unending patience, super-human strength, infinite wisdom.

To be sure, you are wise, patient, and strong. But you're not God. You are a creature. Finite. Limited. Human. Fallible. Welcome to the club.

Somewhere deep in thicket of the book of Exodus, not long after the golden calf episode, God gets really totally done with the stiff-necked, pain-in-the-butt Israelites. God tells Moses to take the people on to the promised land, but without him. I like Moses' response. Moses reminds God that this whole project was God's idea and that these, Yahweh, are "your people." And Moses refuses to go a step without God. God relents.

Do your job, but let God be God, even if that sometimes means prayerfully insisting, as Moses did, that God show up. And, while you're at it, take the rest of the day off.

Sending love . . .

Boundaries

Dear Ones,

Like self-care, boundaries weren't talked about much when I was your age. Then came the clergy sexual abuse crisis. Now we talk about boundaries. Now, clergy in most denominations are required to attend periodic "boundary training" workshops.

It goes without saying, or it should, that sexual abuse and harassment in the church, as elsewhere, must be faced and dealt with clearly and directly. But because many are doing that important work, I want to check in on some other implications of good boundaries.

For me boundaries are about distinguishing between what is my business and what is not my business. To put it another way, what am I responsible for and what belongs to someone else?

As a friend likes to ask, "Does that have your name on it?"

One of the challenges of Christian faith and life in the church is that we do put such great emphasis on compassion, caring for our neighbor, and general concern for others, that it's pretty easy to confuse all that with getting up in other people's business.

There are two problems with taking on things that are not your responsibility. One is that it doesn't work. It is pretty difficult, some would say impossible, for us to change people who aren't interested in changing themselves. The second problem is that if you decide to take on being responsible for someone else's life and business, they get to avoid responsibility for themselves. That's also known as co-dependency.

Just the other day, Laura, your mom spent time listening to a troubled friend who had retired from being the director of an NGO.

Part Two: How Do I Live with This Job?

Though officially retired she continued to give huge amounts of time and energy to her former organization and to monitoring the work of her successor. She said she felt she had to stay this engaged or the organization would lose its way. "Because I was so close to our [now deceased] founder, I am the really only one who can do this." With the best of intentions, she had lost her way and was fast losing her health. And should you find yourself saying, "I am the only one who can do this," think twice. It could be true, but it could be your ego disguised as compassion or duty.

As a pastor you are asked, and properly so, to listen to others and be concerned about their welfare. Such listening can be an enormous help to anyone in sorting out what is going on in order to take the steps they need to take. But it isn't your job to solve other people's problems for them or take on the work that belongs to them. That said, there are times and situations where providing a helping hand is appropriate so that a person gains the strength and leverage to face their own problems.

As a young pastor in a new call, I was constantly hearing from people who said, "The church should be doing this," or "The church should do something about that." I put each concern in my metaphorical backpack, until the day I collapsed under the crushing load of other people's ideas and agendas. And, here's the kicker: I thought I was being a good Christian and pastor by doing this—by taking all this on. What I was doing was getting angry and resentful—not to mention exhausted.

I changed my strategy. When someone said, "I think the church really needs to do this, or that," I would say, "Interesting. Sounds as if you have some passion, some sense of a call, around that. I am happy to support you in taking that on."

Call that "giving responsibility back." For many that was the end of the matter. For a few it was the beginning of a ministry of their own or with others who shared that passion.

Clarity about what is your work and what you are responsible for is "minding your boundaries." You are responsible for doing your work, both your job as a pastor and teacher as well as your own inner work. Others are responsible for doing their work. You may be able to help people get clear about their work, but you can't do it for them.

So that's one application of "boundaries" in the church and ministry that I've found to be important.

Here's another: at one church I served there was an early service in the chapel. After the sermon at this service people were invited to comment on the sermon. One Sunday, a woman who was relatively new to the church and whom I hadn't gotten to know, opened the discussion by saying, "I didn't like anything you said." She then crossed her arms and slumped in her chair in evident disappointment.

As it happened, I wasn't feeling that great about my sermon that day and was probably in a space where I was way too vulnerable (invulnerable and too vulnerable are both problems, extremes to be avoided). In other words, my boundaries weren't in good shape. Her remark devastated me.

Had my boundaries been in better shape I would probably have thought, "Maybe it wasn't a great sermon, still that's a pretty odd thing to say. I wonder what's going on with her?" In other words, I would have had an internal boundary that allowed me a more realistic and less personally damaging response.

I mention this because we are apt to be on the receiving end of harsh, hurtful, or simply bizarre remarks every now and then in the church. It goes with the territory. But we need to have pretty fair boundaries or such remarks can really knock us for a loop.

With better boundaries, I might have said, "Well, I'm sorry you were disappointed by the sermon. Maybe you and I can talk more later? Now, is there someone else who would like to comment?" I would have thought to myself, "Okay, you didn't think it was a great sermon either, but you're doing the best you can right now. Don't get undone. Who knows what's going on with her? There's at least a chance that what she said had a lot more to do with her than with you or your sermon."

To be clear, I am not saying that all criticism can or should be dismissed as someone else's stuff. No, we will receive criticism and sometimes it will be deserved. But we also need to protect ourselves and do a reality check when hurtful remarks come our way.

Part Two: How Do I Live with This Job?

We have to ask, is this criticism accurate? If so, then deal with it. Listen, apologize, move on. Or, is this really about that other person and possibly something I represent to them, but isn't really about me? (By the way, the same thing can happen with praise. If someone is super effusive and seems to think you are God's gift to earth, blinking yellow light there.)

Clergy are human lightning rods. We are targets for a whole lot of projection, i.e., people projecting their own issues, fears, hurts, and hopes onto us. Take legitimate criticism seriously, but don't accept at face value all the stuff that comes your way. Much of the time, it really isn't about you at all. (See above: whose work is this?)

Subsequently, I got to know the woman who spoke up that Sunday. I learned that she didn't have much in the way of filters. Oddly enough, she became a fairly ardent supporter of my ministry. I suspect she has no memory of her remark that day. That I remember it may be a sign that I still have work to do. Like I said, we have all got work—our work—to do. Do your own work, and support others in doing theirs.

Lots more that might be said about boundaries, but that's enough for now.

Sending love . . .

Remaining Faithful Amid Trials

Dear Ones,

I was struggling in my second call church. We had made a big move to take the call and were feeling the loss of a place that was happier and familiar. And I found the new congregation had a lot more grief and conflict in its collective life than I had bargained for.

While most of the congregation were wonderful and supportive (see "How Long Should I Stay?"), in short order I had some serious antagonists. About that time, a friend—also clergy—came to visit. Over a meal I poured out my frustration with the cranks and malcontents. He listened long and hard. Then he said, "If you're doing your job, you are going to make some enemies."

That hit me like the slap of a Zen master. Which is odd, in a way, since it says pretty much that all over the place in the Bible. How had I missed that?

"Blessed are you," said Jesus, "when people revile you and persecute you and utter all kinds of evil against you falsely on my account. Rejoice and be glad, for your reward is great in heaven, for in the same way they persecuted the prophets who were before you." (Matthew 5:11–12)

We tend to think, or at least I thought, "You can't mean me, right, Jesus? I mean, everyone is going to see what a good, smart, caring, trustworthy person/pastor I am and it will all be good."

"That persecution and reviling bit that was like first-century stuff, right?"

Well, no. My friend was right. Jesus was right. Being faithful, doing your job, challenging vested interests, power-grabbers, and preaching the gospel, will make you some enemies. This is a story with a cross in it—remember?

Toward the end of his letter to his youthful protege, Timothy, Paul wrote, "Now you have observed my teaching, my conduct, my aim in life, my faith, my patience, my love, my steadfastness, my persecutions and suffering..." (2 Timothy 3:10–11).

That reads a little like that old Sesame Street routine, "Which of these things doesn't belong here?" It's all going so good, "faith, patience, love, steadfastness" yada, yada, but then "persecutions and suffering." Where did that last bit come from all of a sudden?

Basically, whenever Paul talks about the ministry he's pretty clear: suffering is a part of it.

So, when you ask about "remaining faithful in the midst of trials" this may be a useful place to start. If you are being faithful, you will have trials and make some enemies. Well done! Way to go! Good on ya! High five! Or as Jesus said elsewhere, "In the world you will have tribulation, but be of good cheer, I have overcome the world" (John 16:33).

Such cheerful realism can be helpful. There's a spiritual struggle going on and we can't expect to be exempt from the fray. And if we think the struggle is just "out there," in the wide world, and not in the church, well, we have another think coming.

But this realism is also dangerous. I've known some people who were certain that having everybody mad as hell at them was the sure confirmation of just how righteous, prophetic, and truly faithful they, and usually they alone, were.

So, when facing trials, resistance, and anger, discernment is necessary. Maybe it's because you are being faithful and challenging the powers that be that are perpetuating injustice or faithlessness. But it could be you're the problem, or at least a part of the problem. Maybe some of your words or actions have been unwise or self-serving or just stupid, and the negative feedback has some merit.

You really do have to do some serious discernment in the midst of tests and trials. You need friends like the one to which I poured out my lament. You need colleagues you can trust. Maybe a good therapist. You need to ask yourself honestly, "Have I really been doing any kind of decent self-care or have I let myself get empty and exhausted?"

The trials I have been talking about thus far come as a part of ministry and Christian discipleship. There are, of course, other trials that simply come with being human—illness, death of those we love, financial issues, loneliness, flat tires, and political malpractice. So, more discernment.

I guess what I'd say about ministry is that this is not a sprint; it's a marathon. You have to train for and be prepared for the long haul. Which means, among other things, the hill you are currently climbing won't last forever. I promise.

Sometimes you need to take immediate action to restore perspective, to get some distance on the crap. Take a nap or a walk, a run or a drive. Go on a retreat. Go to the movies. Visit a friend. Call a confidante. Get out of Dodge.

Elijah was a great prophet who had fought the good fight. But, after one good fight and his biggest victory, he was so depleted and empty that he headed for the hills and told God, "Take my life."

When he got to Mt. Horeb, God asked Elijah, "What are you doing here?" Elijah wailed and moaned and said, "I am the only faithful person left in all Israel" (1 Kings 19). He had a pity party. It happens. We get too empty and sad and lonely. We give in to grandiosity. We take ourselves too seriously. "I alone am left," said Elijah.

Actually, no, said God, to the despairing prophet. There are thousands of faithful people left and your next job is to anoint one of them as your successor and help him learn the ropes. Look around. Notice that you aren't alone, that there are all sorts of people doing all sorts of faithful, amazing things. Really.

Should you find yourself feeling alone and thinking "nobody else gets it but me," consider that a flashing yellow, if not a dead red, full stop. Take a break. Get away. Get some distance. Get some laughs. Smell the roses. And then return for the next leg of the marathon.

Sending love . . .

PART THREE

Shop Craft

Starting Out in a New Call

DEAR ONES,
    When I was in seminary I was trying to decide whether to accept a call to a one-year student-pastor position in upstate New York (I was at Union Seminary in NYC). I wanted the experience, but after visiting I told my advisor I wasn't sure these were my people.
    He suggested I put on my "anthropologist's hat." That is, approach the whole thing as if I were studying a fascinating foreign tribe, which they in a way were. They were Scotch-Irish Presbyterians who mostly were trying to survive on small, hard-scrabble farms. While that anthropologist metaphor shouldn't be taken too far, there's something to be said for coming into a new call with a whole lot of curiosity and exercising your best observational powers about your new context.
    A different way to put this is, "use your newness—it won't last long." When you are new to a situation you have permission to be curious and maybe act more naive than you really are, but in a useful way. There's a good chance that your new eyes will enable you to see things that others don't see.
    You can, anthropologist-like, ask innocent questions about how things are done here and why. You can ask people in the congregation to tell you what brought them to the church and what keeps them coming. Pay special attention to what surprises you. Note, too, the behavior of the congregation's leaders. Are they confident? Anxious? Over- or under-functioning?
    This approach is one you can apply to the community where your new church is set as well. Make some time to identify and

Part Three: Shop Craft

talk with community elders about their community. Get to know a realtor and have him/her drive you around and talk about who is moving to town. Develop a relationship with a school counselor or principal to learn about the kids and families there. You get the idea, which is . . . to be curious without (rushing to) judgment. Say, "hmmm . . . how interesting," a lot.

You may have some people who will ask, "What are your plans for us?" Or, "What's your agenda?" Or, "Do you have changes in mind?" Be careful. Probably best to say, sweetly, "Gosh, I just really want to get to know you. I wouldn't presume to announce big plans or make changes, without spending time getting to know you."

Of course, things are different if there's some sort of crisis on arrival or soon after. Like the church has a fire and half the building is gone. Or a church fight breaks out. Or it comes to light that a staff member has been embezzling funds. A crisis will call for calm and deliberation, but also for giving leadership and direction, and more quickly than you might otherwise.

As you begin, building trust is a big part of it. Trust takes time and you never stop working on it. Trust is what allows you to lead and take on the hard stuff. It is the currency of leadership.

How do you build trust? There are three C's: commitment, competence, and character. Commitment means you show up, you're present and engaged. Competence—you do your job with some gifts and reasonable skill. You don't have to be perfect. You don't have to know everything because no one does. (It's a good idea to have one or more experienced, trusted colleagues to call when needed and say, "Help. How do you do this?") The third "C" is character, which is a big bucket. But it essentially means you follow through, you do what you say you'll do, you don't play games or manipulate people, that you are worthy of trust.

Being a good listener helps too. It's a way to practice your curiosity and to build trust. "Tell me about a time when something wonderful happened (in/as church) that you'd love to see more of?" "Tell me about a hard/terrible time that you hope doesn't ever happen again?"

So, be curious—use your new eyes—without rushing to judgment; build trust. And, third, pay attention to what you've heard in the call and start-up process about the congregation's needs and priorities. What are the itches they need scratched?

They may have said, "we need work on stewardship," or "we want our pastor to make hospital calls," or "we need a stronger children's ministry." In most cases, this doesn't mean it's up to you alone, and you shouldn't take on things like stewardship or children's ministry all by yourself. But it is a good idea to indicate that you have been listening and that you want to help address what people think is important.

You may think what they have called out as important misses some key challenges. That's okay. Their time will come. But one of the ways you do build trust is showing that you have been listening. You can even say to your board or leadership, "In my first several months here I've heard a lot of people say (fill in the blank). Does that sound right to you? Here are a couple of ideas I've had about this—help me make them better."

Fourth, a bit of curve ball, be prepared to disappoint people. I don't mean missing a crucial meeting or not showing up when someone is sick or dying. I mean you aren't the Messiah (thankfully, that job has been taken) and when the congregation is waiting for you to walk on water or bring in forty new members who give a lot of money in your first six months, you disappoint unreasonable expectations.

"You want me to help your son find a wife? Not sure I can do that." "You want me to bring back a former member who hasn't been around for ten years? Let's talk about that." "You were hoping I'd be your new best friend? Well, I do want to be your pastor, but that's not quite the same as a friend."

A pastor who tries to meet each and every expectation will end up like a Golden Retriever at a whistler's convention—running in every direction and soon exhausted.

Leadership guru Ron Heifetz quipped in one workshop, "Leadership is disappointing people at a rate they can stand." By which he means that people often expect a new pastor/leader to do all the work for them. "You'll (magically) fix this, right?"

Part Three: Shop Craft

> Leadership doesn't mean that you have the magic bullet. It means that you help people to find the faith and courage to take on their own challenges, and you join them in that work and the adventure.
>
> Sending love...

Praying in Public

Dear Ones,

A part of this topic is your own prayer life. I've shared something about mine in my letter on the spiritual practices that help keep me grounded. In this letter, I want to focus on praying out loud in public or semi-public situations.

Like being at someone's home for a dinner party and at the last moment the host says, "Brittany, would you pray?"

Or when you are on the phone with someone who asks, "Will you pray for me?" "Sure, I'm keep you in my prayers." "No, I mean right now—pray for me."

Or in the hospital, when you are as sad and devastated as everyone else and have no words.

Or when you are at the end of a long meeting, and without warning the person chairing says, "Laura, would you lead us in a closing prayer?"

At least occasionally, you may wish to say, "Do I look like a coin-op prayer machine?" but more likely you just have a deer-in-the-headlights moment of panic as each and every prayerful thought you might have had sets sail and vanishes over the horizon.

To be clear, I do think it is a privilege to pray with and for people, and that this is part of the work of a pastor. And I find it refreshing when, say, having dinner with church folks, the host resists the temptation to call on "the expert" and offers a prayer of their own before the meal.

But still you will be called upon to pray in public without time to prepare—or to lift a great prayer from a book of prayers.

Part Three: Shop Craft

Here are a couple things I've learned.

First, prayer—our prayers—are always the second word. The first word is God's. Our words, and our lives, are a response to God. So, what that means practically is that I usually pause before praying anything aloud at such moments. In the five seconds of silence I draw a breath and ask myself, "What is God saying here?" Or, "What's going on here?" I think of my prayer as a response to God's presence and word among us.

I don't mean to make this too mysterious. Perhaps we've gathered for dinner. What's God doing? Gathering us, calling forth the gift of hospitality, bringing new and old friends together. Or in counseling session, God is enabling our vulnerability, honoring our trust, holding our pain.

This approach also has the value of steering you away from prayer as a performance or being too concerned about a human audience. God is already here, God is already at work, speaking, moving. My word of prayer is in response, the second word. Focus there, on God, not on saying something pretty or cute for audience applause.

Second, it does help to have some opening lines that get things moving in the right, that is a Godward, direction. The Psalms, which I tend to think of as a school of prayer, offer some good ones.

"O God, whose mercy is from everlasting to everlasting . . ." (Psalm 90:2) is a good starter. Or, "Lord, you who have been our dwelling place in all the generations . . ." (Psalm 90:1). "O God, whose steadfast love endures forever . . ." comes from Psalm 136. Beyond the psalms, something like this, "Jesus, you have said to us 'Come to me all you who are weary and heavy-laden and I will give you rest . . .'" You get the idea. Let the psalms and Scripture shape your prayers and your language of prayer. Have a couple of lines like this up your sleeve, to get you started.

Third, there's not a thing wrong with committing a couple wonderful, classic prayers to memory and praying those when they are appropriate to the moment. (We aren't called to be original so much as faithful.) Sometimes I just pray by reciting Psalm 23 or Psalm 121.

The other type of praying in public you are called on to do is different. It is in leading the church in worship. For this you usually have time to prepare, and you should—prepare, that is. Giving time and attention to preparing our prayers is important.

Why? Well, partly we ought to want to do our best, knowing that we won't always manage it and that's okay. But there's another reason to pay attention to our praying in worship. Part of what's going there is that we are teaching people to pray. We don't do that directly or didactically, but indirectly by example and experience.

As a young pastor, I found it helpful to devote some time to sorting out for myself the different kinds of prayer—adoration, praise, confession, lament, thanksgiving, intercession, petition, blessing—and to prepare prayers for worship of those types that fit with the different parts and movement of the service.

Sometimes a prayer would be written out for all of us to pray together. Other times it would be something prayed by a pastor or a worship leader. Or there is "bidded" prayer, where you give a prompt, e.g. "Let us pray for those known to us who stand today in special need of God's grace," followed by silence for people's prayers.

It used to be a convention to have a longish "pastoral prayer" in worship and probably still is some places. But in a lot of churches these days there's a new normal for prayer. That is to pass a microphone and let people offer their own prayers and concerns.

While this can be truly and deeply prayerful, it can also go awry. Sometimes these "prayers" sound more like announcements. Also, some people seem to find the prospect of an available microphone about the way an alcoholic regards a cocktail. You hear from them every week.

Sometimes this format just feels a bit small, even, dare I say it, trivial. That is, we focus a lot on very personal things as well as a litany of specific health concerns (grandma's broken hip, uncle Tom's next round of chemo) but miss fulsome adoration, deep lament, or robust praise. We tend, it seems, to focus more on us and less on the majesty, might, and mercy of God.

If this is the format that predominates, what are some things a worship leader can do to enrich it? Rather than inviting prayers per se, invite the sharing of joys and concerns for prayer. Take brief notes as these are shared, and then as a worship leader, weave these into a prayer. This can be the best of both worlds.

Another option is to do a class or sermon series on prayer. Explore the different types of prayer. Or study the psalms. Spend some time together both praying and writing prayers that may subsequently be used in a service. The idea is to deepen without inhibiting.

Or use this pass-the-mic format sometimes, but vary it with other options, such as inviting one layperson to prepare prayers of thanksgiving and intercession with the theme of the service in mind. Or, as I mentioned earlier, use a "bidded" prayer format.

To be part of a congregation that prays deeply and authentically, whether led by a pastor, or in some other form, is a wonderful and powerful thing. It is something to seek, with God's help. It is something to pray for.

Sending love . . .

Relationships with Colleagues

Dear Ones,

Colleagues . . . good colleagues . . . are a huge gift, not to be taken for granted. Tell them you appreciate them. Do nice things for them. Pray for them. Colleagues who are difficult are a definite trial. But this happens, more often than you would like to think. Pray for them too.

There's a lot to this topic. So, let's make two letters of it. This first one will be more general, though including a couple thoughts specific to your present role as "Associate Ministers."

The second letter will focus more on personnel issues. This is one of those things that is not taught in seminary, and probably shouldn't be, maybe can't be. But it is definitely one to ramp up on once on the job. I imagine that in a year or two, or five, you, dear Brittany and Laura, will likely be lead ministers or solo pastors with responsibility for personnel stuff. Not glamorous, but it can do you in if you aren't paying attention.

So, we will return to that personnel-head-of-staff stuff. For now, some more general remarks on relationships with colleagues.

Relationships with one's colleagues on a church staff are pressurized. You spend a fair amount of time together. You depend on each other. You see the best and worst of each other. And, all the while, there is a whole congregation of people observing your interactions. Even if most pay little attention, you are in a fishbowl of sorts.

In such a pressurized environment fellow staff members are likely to bring out what's inside of us. They may call forth our idealism, energy, and love. And they may also call forth our anger, envy, lust, or other particular wounds we bear. That is to say, they are in a good position to trigger us.

Should you find a particular colleague getting under your skin, take a step back and ask yourself, as bravely and honestly as you can manage, "What is going on with me? What in me is getting triggered by her (him)?" A somewhat different way to put this (with broader application) is, "When it gets hard, get curious."

I'm not saying, "it's all about you." But feeling triggered, getting emotionally charged, usually means that some of it is about you. When you have some clarity and calm around your stuff, you stand a better chance of dealing with the other person. It may be good to explore these things with a spiritual director or therapist or another confidant.

The prospect of involving a third person leads to a topic that is a challenge for our interactions on a church staff and in the church: triangulation. You know what that is. Three people a triangle makes. Let's call them X, Y, and Z. Say X has an issue with Z. But instead of dealing directly with Z, X talks about Z with Y. Triangulation. (Triangulation is also possible around issues, like an addiction. Z has an addiction. Y is the addiction. X takes on responsibility for dealing with the addiction [Y], thus relieving Z of his own work.)

There are a lot of problems with triangulation. One is that, if you are X you are highly unlikely to resolve your issues with Z by talking about Z to other people. Moreover, there's something just a little yucky about this. It is talking about someone behind their back. Often it is griping or whining. Sometimes it is worse— "bearing false witness" as it is called in Scripture.

Another problem with triangulation is that X may be trying to get Y to take on responsibilities that don't belong to Y. "Would you talk to Z for me?" Or Y, may —unwisely—offer to take on X's work here. "Would you like me to talk to Z for you?"

All that said about the dangers of triangulation, there are some times when triangulation is permissible, even a really good idea.

Say you are X and you have an issue with Z. Y, as it happens, has been around for a while and knows Z far better than you. So, you might talk with Y and say, "I'm not sure how best to bring this up with Z. Based on your experience, what you would suggest?" Or

Relationships with Colleagues

you might say to Y, "Can I talk with you about what happened in that meeting with Z for a reality check? Here's what I think happened. I'd be interested to know if you saw it the same or differently."

These seem to me to be reasonable triangulations, so to speak. I sometimes tell people, "You're allowed two triangulations. After that you've got to deal with Z." These two are for this kind of stuff. But it can't go on and on that X talks with you (Y) about Z. Two's my limit.

There's another situation when triangulation is appropriate. If X does not feel safe alone with Z. Then you may come up with a plan whereby Y, or some other third party, sits in as X talks with Z.

But otherwise triangulation is the bane of church life. It happens a lot because being direct entails risk and takes courage. And lots of times in church we place too high a value on being "nice," and think that being direct is "not nice." Actually, I think it is far nicer to be direct (see Matthew 18:15-20). Talking maliciously behind someone's back is what's not nice.

There will always be some members of a congregation who will want to triangulate you. When you are an associate minister some will try to triangulate you against the lead or senior minister or another colleague. Such folks tend to come on a bit like the serpent in the garden. Subtle, clever, and seductive.

Such a person may drop by your office and after warming you up by saying how great your recent sermon was may add, "I was just wondering, are you as uncomfortable with the decision Z has made on this as I am?" or "I'm sure glad there's someone on the staff (i.e., you) who really understands us (not like Z)." DO NOT TAKE THE BAIT.

If someone has an issue with the senior minister or another person on the staff, encourage them to talk to that person. If the person appears genuine and fair, you may listen, as noted above, on a limited basis to clarify. But that is so that they can have a direct, productive conversation. Beyond that be careful.

In my view, associate ministers owe it to the head of staff to be loyal and supportive of that person. That doesn't mean you can't disagree. But if you do disagree, express yourself directly, in private, or, when appropriate, within a staff meeting. Do not air your issues

Part Three: Shop Craft

out in public. Do not triangulate with members of the congregation. Do not express yourself in passive-aggressive nonverbal ways like looking bored out of your mind or doing the *New York Times* crossword puzzle during that person's sermon.

If you have an issue with the lead/senior minister and their leadership, talk to them directly. If you find, over time, that you cannot respect that person, update your profile and start your job search.

Finally, it helps always to be clear about what is your work (business) and what is not, and to focus on the stuff that is yours.

In churches people sometimes like to play "bunch ball." Remember little kids playing soccer? Everyone runs to the ball and stands in a pack flailing away. Shins get hurt, but the ball often doesn't move at all. The idea in soccer is to play your position so that team members have someone to pass the ball to. Your team might even score a goal. This analogy works pretty well in church too. Play your position and support others in playing theirs.

Sending love . . .

Meetings, Meetings, Meetings

Dear Ones,

There are a lot of meetings as part of church life, aren't there?

Can they be better? Can we do a meaning-infusion, a depth-charge if you will, into our meetings? Some meetings are good, but too many float on the surface where they are imperiled by minutiae and personal pettiness.

I have a couple of strategies for change, but first let me share an understanding of our work that has been meaningful to me.

It is the rabbinic model of ministry. Rabbis are thought of as community or field-based scholars and teachers. I love that. When I was weighing my call and career options there were really two: university teaching or the ministry. I felt called to teach, but in a different context than the college or university. I wanted to be more engaged in daily life and with people in all the ages and stages of life. The ministry has been a great fit.

Except for this. In the church, too, we compartmentalize. Teaching happens, we assume, in church school and adult education classes. Meetings are about tasks, programs, and administration. Mission is about mission, and so on.

Really? I think that, especially in our new post-Christendom time, everything the church does teaches. How we show up in worship teaches. How we relate to people at the margins teaches something about who Christians are and what they believe. How we read and use Scripture in worship often says more about what we believe about it than any doctrine of biblical inspiration.

So, I asked if serving on a church board could be part of our faith-formation ministry? I suggested that those who accepted such a call to serve ought to be able to expect that the experience would be one of growing in faith.

I thought serving on a board or committee could—and should—include growing in faith as part of the experience. We promised people that. It wasn't all about you giving and doing. You would also receive something: a deepened faith, deepened relationships.

How to deliver on that?

Here is one strategy that proved pretty successful (in a second letter related to this I will discuss another strategy).

Have a board or committee or ministry team build into their meeting some "study time." Something that relates to their mission and ministry, to why they were there and what they were trying to do. This takes us deeper, beyond the level of all the tasks on their plate.

So, let's say it's the Board of Parish Care and Fellowship. We might take Dietrich Bonhoeffer's little classic, *Life Together*, which is all about Christian community and koinonia. Allocate twenty minutes at the beginning of each meeting to discussing that month's reading, one chapter of the book each month.

As the minister, that is to say a "pastor and teacher," you might lead that portion of the meeting. Don't lecture. Do involve people in engaging what they've read. Ask people to share a passage from the book that spoke to them. Invite them to ponder and share their thoughts on how what Bonhoeffer is saying might relate to something on the evening's agenda. Or share the leadership among board members. You can offer to check in a week before the meeting with the person who will lead that month's conversation and help them plan for it.

Variations on this theme: instead of a book, select biblical passages that are relevant to the board's mission. Take a *lectio divina* approach, reading the passage aloud and inviting people to share words or phrases that speak to them. Then invite them to share what they hear God saying to them through this passage about the work that we share in this board. Use a "no-crosstalk" approach (more on that in the second part of this letter).

Another alternative to a book or biblical passages might be germane articles. Magazines like *The Christian Century* or *Sojourners*, or websites like Alban or Lewis Center for Church Leadership or Faith and Leadership at Duke are good places to scan regularly for articles that deepen our conversation and experience.

So that's the idea: build in a depth-charge and team building related to the mission and work of a board, committee, or ministry team.

Some will resist. "We've got too much to do." "We have to get on with the agenda." Ask them to suspend disbelief, to try it as an experiment for a season or a year, and then evaluate. My experience with this sort of thing is that it grounds people and builds relationships in a way that makes the rest of the meeting more focused and productive.

In conclusion to this first letter on your suggested topic of "how to bring theology into meetings," let me return to my starting point. You, as an ordained minister, are a teacher of the faith and a center of theological integrity for your congregation. So even if the idea of a study/conversation doesn't fly, you still have the opportunity and responsibility to bring a theological perspective to a board or committee with which you are working.

That need not mean a big theological debrief. It might as simple as, "You know, I was thinking about our last meeting and a story from the Bible that came to mind was that one about Martha and Mary. You know how that goes? Does that shed any light on what we're struggling with?"

I have sometimes played a role at a church conference or denominational meeting called "theological reflector." As the "TR," you are on for five to seven minutes at the end of each business session to frame things theologically and put them in that perspective. I found it a fun task that can be adapted to other meetings.

Sending love . . .

Inviting God to the Meeting

Dear Ones,

Your instinct to add depth to meetings is sound for all sorts of reasons. For one thing, when groups operate only at the level of tasks to be done, they tend to burn out. Our work is funded, energetically, by going deeper, getting in touch with deeper stories of our faith.

The previous letter proposed one way to get in touch with the deep stories. Here's another. One deep story come from our own Congregational/United Church of Christ heritage. The story of "The People of the Meeting."

The early Congregationalists were known as "People of the Meeting." Their churches were called "Meeting Houses." This was not because they had endless meetings. It was because they believed that when the church gathered it was in order to meet and be met by the living God. The Meeting House was named that because it was where you encountered God. "Going to meeting," an old-timey expression for going to church, meant going to meet the Lord.

For the early Congregationalists, there wasn't as much difference between worship and a church meeting as there seems to be now. Both meant being in the presence of the living God.

Is God a part of our meetings these days? Or is the prayer at the beginning of a meeting a time when we say, in effect, "Thank you God, and you may now be excused"?

If so, how do we recover the deep practice of our forebears? Well, here's a start. For early Congregationalists the point of a meeting wasn't chiefly to determine the will of the majority (i.e., what we want), it was to seek the mind of Christ (i.e., what God wants).

Inviting God to the Meeting

You may want to read that over again. As simple as it sounds, it is actually a Really Big Deal. It is "radical" in the actual meaning of the word, which is to "go back to the roots." (For more on this see my *Transforming Congregational Culture* and the chapter, "From Democracy to Discernment.")[5]

With such a shift, we might spend less time and energy trying to line up votes for our side or to convince the other side that we are right, and spend more time in seeking the mind of Christ and the guidance of the Holy Spirit. I particularly found this applicable to congregational meetings, like the church annual meeting.

So how do you actually do this? There are no fool-proof methods or techniques. The Spirit blows where it wills, as Jesus said. But here are a couple I like.

First, add time and space in a meeting for prayer and for silence. Give permission to people to request a break in debate and deliberations, at any time, for prayer.

A second idea, when you have a decision to make or a contentious issue to face, is to create a safe place in which people can share their heart and mind on the topic without fear of censure or judgment. I like the "No Crosstalk" approach used in twelve-step groups. Each person gets to say what they have to say, but other people do not comment on or respond to what has been said. They do not address the speaker directly. (And watch those nonverbals too. A frown or a sigh can say a lot.) Those who listen get to say, "Thank you." Then the next person has their chance. Sometimes listening to each other in this way becomes a way of listening for the Holy Spirit.

Or, third, when taking a vote on something, instead of asking for, "All in favor," and "all against" ask, "If you sense God's leading in this motion, please signify by saying yes." And the other side of the coin, "If you do not sense God's leading in the motion, please signify by saying no." Framing it that way can get people to pause for what may be a crucial moment and reframe their voting.

Finally, be open to the idea that the Spirit has a different timetable than we do. We may feel a decision has to be made right now,

---

5. Robinson, *Transforming Congregational Culture*, 92–99.

tonight. Maybe not. If we are unsettled and do not feel that we have clear guidance, we may decide to wait, to wait until we can say, as in Acts 15, "It seemed good to us and to the Holy Spirit." Sometimes you have to wait on the Spirit.

In conclusion to both these letters on theological infusion (transfusion?) for church meetings, either of these shifts, whether to add "study time" and faith formation to a board meeting, or to recover a Congregational sense of our meetings as a time when we seek the mind of Christ—will take time and persistence on your part and that of other leaders. These are changes in the culture. They don't happen in a month or two. They take time, maybe two or three years to really get into the system. So, if you embark on such a path don't give up too soon.

Sending love . . .

Is There a Word from the Lord?

DEAR ONES,

In my lifetime preaching, or the sermon, has been declared "dead" about every ten years or so. Still, it persists. Why? I think Paul was right. Faith comes by hearing. "So faith comes from what is heard, and what is heard comes through the word of Christ" (Romans 10:17).

It's an amazing thing, the sermon, the power of the spoken word to reach inside us, to create a new reality that did not previously exist, until it is spoken into being.

Preaching is also hard work. Early in my ministry I came across this, which I found heartening: "Preaching well is a great labor. That is the chief reason it does not happen very often. It requires too much of us . . . The chief hazard to effective preaching is having a gift with words. Strong, silent types for whom words are wrung like so many drops of blood have the advantage here. Their need to get a thing straight in their heads before they presume to say it is the people's best assurance."[6]

I found that heartening because I did find preaching a great labor. I worked hard at it, and sometimes failed, though we need to be cautious about judging our sermons as "successes" or "failures." This is one of those places where, in Isaiah's words, "God's ways are not our ways."

---

6. Sloyan, *Worshipful Preaching*, 3.

Here's a bit about how I go about preaching. It's not the only way. It may not be yours, but perhaps you'll glean something of value from my experience.

For me, good preaching begins with good listening. Preachers listen to many voices, but what we are listening for is God's word, which more often than not comes indirectly rather than directly.

For me, the listening that precedes speaking that is a sermon, is first of all listening to Scripture. I start there. Mostly I have been a lectionary preacher, working with the appointed lessons for a given Sunday. That seemed to me a way of keeping a preacher, and a congregation, honest. You had to deal with stuff you have not chosen, may not like, or find easy to comprehend. I can't tell you how many times texts that seemed initially off-putting have yielded my better sermons. (You may also need to familiarize your congregation with the concept of a lectionary and the experience of your text being given more than chosen.)

But listening means you have to shut up. You have to put on hold those voices of your own that already know what this text is saying. You have to resist the clamoring voice of your own agenda and superimposing it on the text. What is the text saying? What is God saying though the text?

You don't entirely silence yourself, of course. In addition to the Scripture, your own true voice is one to which you listen as well. You also listen to your community, the congregation, it's song of joy and sorrow. And the world, with its myriad happenings and cacophony.

And what you listen for is a word from God. I've always thought the antique-sounding question, "Is there a word from the Lord?" a good one. We preachers get to listen for that word and then to bear it back as wet, hard to hold, and translucent as a just-caught trout.

Besides the "Is there a word from the Lord" question, there are a couple other questions that I try to keep in mind as I ponder a text.

"What's at stake?" is one of those. What's going on here and why does it matter? That drives you to the exegetical tasks of paying attention to the context of the text, to the urgent life issues in play then, and by analogy, now.

Too many sermons I hear sound to me as if little or nothing is at stake, which if true is damning. A mentor of mine spoke of preaching as "breaking open the Word of God." That sort of violent language seems right. You are messing here with something powerful, something potent.

Another question I like to ask is, "What's wrong with this text?" I probably ought to put "wrong" in quotes. The idea isn't what is factually "wrong," so much as what is disturbing or weird or provocative. We can get so committed to the idea of the Bible's sweet sanctity that we miss the rough edges, the tensions, the push and pull. We miss the shock of the gospel.

Like Jesus saying, "I have come not to call the righteous but sinners," or the bizarre overkill at Cana when Jesus produces something on the order of 6,500 bottles of wine, or him asking in the parable of the workers in the vineyard, "you got a problem with that?" when our honest answer is, "I sure as hell do."

I have almost always written out my sermons word for word. For me that is part of "getting a thing straight in my head." But I don't read them. I see what I've written sort of like a script in a play. Which also means that things other than words are at work. Like silence between words. Or gestures and facial expressions. Like listening to the unspoken dialogue that is going on. What is the congregation saying back to you in the unspoken dialogue as you preach? What is the congregation saying with its body language, its faces and its energy?

After the listening and the writing, there is the doing, the preaching. For this I developed three "rules." These I recall in the hour or so before preaching, when I also ask God to anoint me with the Holy Spirit and use me as an instrument of his grace.

Rule Number One: Trust Your Calling. There's a reason you're here, that you are in the pulpit today. Sure, you can think of better preachers, but for right now and right here, you are the one God has called. Trust that.

Rule Number Two: Trust Your Words. The stuff you've written, put down. Edit the hell out of it. Divert from it at the direction of the Holy Spirit. But trust these words you have been given. They may not look like much, marks on paper (or your iPad) but you gotta trust your material.

Rule Number Three: Enjoy Yourself. Okay, so not every Sunday is up, not every sermon joyful. There are hard topics and tragic days. But overall, there's a joy in this. The joy of being a bearer of good news. The joy of speaking of God in the midst of God's people. Have joy in it. Remember, no joy for the preacher, no joy for the congregation.

I also do some stretching to limber up my whole body, and I sing a bit to get my mouth and vocal chords warmed up. It is a whole body experience and how you use your body matters hugely.

As I left my last church, a man said to me, "I never came to you for pastoral care or counseling in all these years, but in every one of your sermons I felt cared for." I was touched. Preaching is a great labor, but also a great privilege. Give it your best and then give it up to God.

Sending love . . .

Leadership

Dear Ones,

Leadership has become a hot topic in recent years. Why? Congregations have been complaining to seminaries that they need pastors who are leaders, but they aren't getting them.

That said, it is also true that when congregations actually get a leader not everyone will be pleased. Leaders make a difference. They ask hard questions. They don't always tell people what they want to hear. At one congregation I served, a consultant reported to the church council, "Your pastoral search committee was told they need to get a leader. They got one. Not everyone is happy with that."

So, what are we talking about when we talk about leadership? What is it? What do leaders do?

I think of leadership as a function, rather than a status or even a position. It is something some person or group or team does to help a congregation or other organization be more faithful and fruitful.

Some equate leadership with status, being more important than other people. Or they think a leader is someone who occupies a leadership position. But a person may occupy a leadership position or hold a certain status and not be a leader at all. Leadership is most of all a function.

And that function is to help a congregation identify and engage its own most pressing problems and important challenges.

Which means that authentic leaders don't arrive with all the answers or with a predetermined vision or agenda. They pay attention. They listen. They try to get an accurate picture of reality.

From that they identify, and help others identify, the key challenges facing a church. What is the urgent work God has placed before us at this time?

Such challenges are not always what people initially think they are. I've worked with many congregations that were pretty convinced their big challenge was "getting new members."

That strikes me as more of a symptom than the real challenge. More often the deeper challenge is a lack of clarity or passion about a congregation's purpose or mission. Why are we here and what are we trying to be and do? Congregations that are reasonably clear and excited about their core purpose tend to be interesting and exciting to others.

So just because people say, "This is our biggest challenge" doesn't mean they've really gotten to the heart of the thing. Naming our challenges accurately takes work and it takes time. When you've got a handle on what is before you, then the leadership task is mobilizing people to engage those key challenges.

But before we get too far along, let me post a warning. Flashing light here: leadership is dangerous. Ron Heifetz, who teaches at the Kennedy School at Harvard, and whose work has influenced me a lot, writes, "You appear dangerous to people when you question their values, beliefs and habits of a lifetime. You place yourself on the line when you tell people what they need to hear rather than what they want to hear. Although you may see with clarity and passion, a promising future of progress and gain, people will see with equal passion the losses you are asking them to sustain."[7]

I mention this because you may be doing a terrific job of leadership and find that not everyone is thrilled. Doing the job well doesn't mean the job is easy or that you will win a popularity contest. (But, this doesn't mean the opposite is true, i.e. people are upset ergo, I must be doing a great job. Sorry, but no.)

So, to review, first, leadership is function (not a status), second, the function is help a congregation accurately name and engage its most pressing problems and important challenges, and, third, this work can be tough and dangerous.

---

7. Heifetz and Linsky, *Leadership on the Line*, 12.

It is also absolutely necessary. Those congregations that have been saying to seminaries "we need leaders" are not wrong. Without energetic and effective leaders, churches, as well as other organizations, tend to spend a lot of time and energy going nowhere.

Worse, just like nature churches abhor a vacuum. A leadership vacuum will be filled. But often those who move to fill such a vacuum are, in my experience, motivated by their own needs for power and recognition (of which they are mostly unaware). Worse, they are rarely accountable to anyone. Here be dragons, so to speak.

Okay, so how do you go about it? This thing called "leadership"?

Step one (which is never finished) is building trust. Trust is the currency of leadership. You gain trust by doing your job and doing it reasonably well. You gain trust by building relationships. And you gain trust by following through on what you have said you will do. (Don't make promises that you can't or won't follow through on.)

One of life's sad little ironies is that building trust takes a long time; destroying it can be done more or less overnight. Doesn't seem fair, but that's the way it is.

Step two is defining reality. As a person who is new to a church (or other organization), be curious. Look for patterns. Look at the parts and the whole, and how they fit together (or don't). Listen for the story this congregation tells about itself. This is that "getting to the balcony" I mentioned way back in the introduction. Congregations don't always have a very clear picture of their own reality or of the context/community where they are. Getting a reasonably accurate picture of what's going on is important.

Step Three: set a direction/priorities. This will reflect the second step picture of reality and the identification of the key challenges. Working with your colleagues and lay leaders, set a direction. Call it "taking the next step" or "writing the next chapter in our story." Don't take on too much. Focus on a couple of key things.

Step Four is hang in there. If you are working on real stuff there will be pushback. You'll probably discover the need for some course corrections, but beware of losing focus on the main goals or directions. Heifetz says good leaders "maintain disciplined attention." And since most important work takes three to five years, don't give up too soon.

Part Three: Shop Craft

So that's an overview of the nature and work of leadership as I think about it.

I want to do a follow-up letter in which I explore a really helpful distinction for which Ron Heifetz has become somewhat famous. I actually think Jesus was onto it a few years earlier than that.

Sending love . . .

Prophetic Leadership

Dear Ones,

The feeding of the 5,000 is one of the relatively few stories that makes it into all four of the Gospels. As is often true, John's version (found in John 6) is markedly different from the other three Gospels.

In the Gospel of John the bread and fish miracle is not a compassion story, as it mostly is in the synoptic Gospels of Matthew, Mark, and Luke. It is a revelation story. God is revealed in this sign of many thousand being fed from a ridiculously small amount. Do the people get it? As in, do they see that God is at work, that God is in their midst? No, they hunt Jesus down to get more bread. He stops them in their tracks, saying, "You are looking for me not because you saw the sign, but because you ate your fill of the bread."

Instead of more bread, Jesus gives them a challenge: "to do the work of God." When they ask what that might be, he answers, "Believe in the one whom God has sent." They want a fixer who will do it for them. He asks of them engagement, commitment, and a faith that risks.

This story anticipates a really helpful distinction that Ron Heifetz has developed in relation to the nature of leadership. There's a difference, says Heifetz, between a "technical problem" and an "adaptive challenge."[8] The difference parallels what happens in John 6. The people think they've got a technical problem: no bread. They call in an expert/authority whose job it is to fix the problem.

---

8. Heifetz and Linsky, *Leadership on the Line*, 14.

Part Three: Shop Craft

Jesus sees it differently. He sees what Heifetz calls adaptive work, work the people need to do. That work involves risk, learning, growing, trust, and change on their part.

Because we live in a society that has had such great technical success, we are apt to view most every challenge as a technical problem. Get the right expert who applies the right technique, and voila, problem solved!

So, say the church believes it needs more members who will give money so it can make its budget. Solution: get a minister who will draw them in. That may (or may not) work. But even if a new minister does draw some new folks in, they won't stay or really become part of things unless the congregation also does its own work.

To adapt Heifetz's language even more to the church setting, I think you could call the work of the technical problems "priestly," while adaptive work and leadership are more "prophetic." The priest has an answer to a problem. Say this prayer. Do this ritual.

The prophet has questions: Are we being faithful? Are we willing to get out of our comfort zone? What about this gap between what we say and what we do? There is place for both: solving technical problems and leading adaptive work. But I think of leading adaptive work as intrinsically spiritual in nature because it asks people to take risks, to experience change of mind and heart and to grow in faith.

Heifetz goes on to say that "leadership failure" happens when we treat adaptive challenges as technical problems. I had some experience of that as a young pastor. I thought that if I just worked harder and was a super pastor and preacher, the church would spring to life. What I found was I got really tired, tired and resentful.

The real task is to give the work back to the people. The trick is give the work back at a rate they can stand.

For a long time, mainline religious leaders have thought of prophets as mainly being about social justice and engaging political powers. Prophet Nathan calling King David to account. Martin Luther King challenging America to live up to its ideals. Jim Wallis calling racism America's "original sin."

While that certainly has a place, the problem with thinking that this societal focus is what "prophetic ministry" is all about is we overlook the responsibility of leaders/clergy to be prophetic in and to the community of faith, i.e. the church.

Jesus mostly directed his prophetic challenge exactly there—to his community of faith, Judaism. He really wasn't focused on getting the Romans to be nicer tyrants. He didn't spend a lot of time picketing Herod's palace or organizing letter writing campaigns to Caesar.

So—cutting to the chase—we need a lot more pastors to be prophets, not just to the wider culture or to political leaders, but to their own congregation, to the church. And that doesn't mean saying, "Hey, you guys are racists." It means challenging the church to be more faithful and fruitful.

Prophetic leadership means asking the questions that are sort of the elephant-in-the-room variety. "Why are we here?" "What's our purpose?" "What are we trying to do?" "Who are we serving, and who are we called to serve?" "How have we confused being the church and being a club?"

In these days of mainline shrinkage many churches have morphed into something that resembles a club. (And the church building a clubhouse.) In the church qua club, the main purpose becomes the comfort and satisfaction of the members. This may be jolly, but it is not the church of Jesus Christ. The church, bottom line, is about changing lives. Prophetic leaders remind the church that it is not a club for the benefit of the members, but a community that participates in God's mission in and for the world.

Prophetic leadership is only possible when a minister has also done her pastoral and priestly work. If you haven't sat at the kitchen table to listen or by the hospital bed to pray during the week, you have no business standing in the pulpit on Sunday with a word of challenge.

Too many clergy get the pastor/priest part—serving felt needs, providing religious goods and services, keeping things going (which is important and necessary)—but it is not leavened with prophetic leadership. This includes asking good questions, challenging assumptions, asking "why do we do things this way?" "Tell me again, why our church is sponsoring a golf tournament?"

Why has prophetic ministry in and to the congregation gone missing? My hunch: too many clergy think their job description is to be "Rev. Nice," to be the most loving, patient, caring person in the known world. But this job is more complicated, interesting, and dangerous than that. It's a both/and. Loving people and challenging them—even as our faith and God do both, love us and challenge us. (Sometimes the very best way to share a challenge with people is to let them know how challenged you find yourself to be.)

As you practice leadership, John 6 and the Heifetz "technical problem/adaptive challenge" are good to keep in mind (and John 6 isn't the only biblical illustration of this. Scripture is actually chock-full of adaptive work, e.g. the whole exodus/wilderness story).

It's easy to get sucked into doing, or trying to do, everything for people, to attempt to dazzle them. But real growth in faith occurs when, with your support and guidance, people take on their work themselves. Jesus didn't, after all, say, "Watch me," he said, "Follow me."

Sending love . . .

How Long Should I Stay?

Dear Ones,
Here's the question: how long should a minister stay in a particular pastoral call?

I've wrestled with this. And, as a consultant and coach, I found many of my clergy clients struggled with it. As the band, The Clash, put it, "Should I Stay or Should I Go?"

"How long should I stay?" is a tough question and an important one. It matters for you, for your family, for your congregation. It matters to Jesus. There are no easy answers. A bunch of different factors bear on the question—your age, your family situation and needs, your energy and fatigue, and yes, your best sense of what God is asking of you, calling you to at any given time. Another factor is whether you are a solo pastor, a lead pastor, or in a staff position. My experience has been in the first two and my comments reflect that.

Acknowledging the many variables, there are a couple of generalizations I can offer that may be helpful.

One is that it just takes time to build trust and relationships as a minister. A bit of conventional wisdom, that has seemed to me more or less true, is that it takes a new minister five years to become the pastor of the church. That is both a long time and a short time. Moreover, it is weird because it is at odds with so much else in our culture.

We live a world where things move very fast, where companies reinvent themselves and people change jobs often. Ministry is different. It takes time. Unless you are doing a new church start, chances are good that you are part of the "slow church" movement in a "fast food," "instant gratification" world.

Part Three: Shop Craft

This has further implications. You may get impatient in years two or three. You feel wholly present and committed, but you're not sure the congregation is at the same place. Probably they are not. It takes time and shared experience.

But there's another thing about the early years. After some initial honeymoon phase, you are likely—if you're doing your job—to encounter some headwinds, pushback, or obstacles. The early years, rewarding in their way, can also be the very hardest. So, changing positions every three years, as many clergy do, may mean you are chasing the courtship and honeymoon high. Or that you just aren't too bright because you keep doing the hardest stretch over and over again without getting to the pay-off.

In my experience, years seven to twelve were often among the most productive and satisfying. They were also ones in which I was freer to focus on the things I did best.

It is also true that longer pastorates are generally better for congregations. Just as the pastor who moves too often is doing the demanding on-boarding over and over in new situations, so a congregation expends a lot of energy in search, interim, start up, learning their new pastor, etc.

It may also happen that another church or recruiter approach you, asking you to consider their job. Be careful, that can be very seductive. The suitors are on their best behavior and may be telling you "You're the one," while back at the ranch, so to speak, life in the congregation you are serving is challenging and it has been a good long while before anyone there seemed to be going out of their way to tell you how glad they are that you are there. There are some analogies to having a marital affair.

Can you stay too long? Definitely. I've seen way too many clergy who after twenty years in one place were some version of RIP (retired in place). A congregation will tolerate that for a while. But eventually they lose patience and what was once a good ministry often ends badly.

Beyond these observations about patterns of tenure, here's one more general comment.

Most clergy encounter some resistance. We experience some people who, for whatever reason, take an adversarial position. The worst can make life hell. (See "Bullying.") The best may have something important to teach you. We do well to listen and attempt to discern what is true from what is false.

But the tendency of many clergy is to turn the volume way up on the negative voices—kind of like practicing the total opposite of appreciative inquiry (where the approach is to ask, "what's going well?"). A single complaint is held fast, while a stream of compliments dribble away, discounted.

My point? Say you're getting pushback. And, say, it is hurtful. And that it's not fair. Then you may find yourself saying, "Enough of this crap," activate your job search or write your "'f— you' letter of resignation."

What clergy in such a situation tend not to notice is the large majority of the congregation love and appreciate them. They support you. But they aren't as noisy or as constant as the nay-sayers. Listen, you never get 100 percent.

There's a danger that we listen too much to the nay-sayers and don't listen at all to the other folks who, sadly, may not be saying much because they are happy. So, we get a distorted picture of reality. And then we make a decision to explore other positions or leave, based on that skewed perception.

So, just saying, in weighing how long to stay, don't act from a distorted picture of reality born of hurt and frustration. Try to get an accurate picture of the situation.

Understand that if you are doing your job, you will make some enemies. Remember, sometimes our detractors have a point. We aren't perfect. Often, however, such folks are grumpy or bitter for reasons that have little or nothing to do with you. Or they really are bullies. Their resistance doesn't mean you're doing a crap job. In fact, it may mean just the opposite (see: crucifixion).

So, in assessing how long to stay, be careful about listening to the wrong voices. Create some spaces where you can listen, most of all, for God's voice.

Sending love . . .

PART FOUR

Tough Stuff

Personnel Issues

Dear Ones,

As noted in the earlier letter on the topic of relationships with colleagues, you are likely to be in the role of lead pastor or head-of-staff for some fortunate congregation before too long.

With that prospect in mind, here are some thoughts about how the personnel systems in the church work and don't work, and might be made to work somewhat better. No, nothing glamorous about this work, but if you don't pay attention it can come back to bite you. I can show you my bite marks!

And the personnel system of a church has a good deal to do with our relationships with others on a church staff. Particularly if we are the head of staff, it is this system that sets us up for success or failure, productivity, or problems.

Why do I say that about a bunch of bureaucratic/administrative stuff? Can it really be that important? Yes.

Too often churches are places where personnel issues and the nature of relationships between members of a staff are, in a word, fuzzy. Now, fuzzy can work just fine if everyone you are working with is a totally mature adult human. But we cannot really count on that, so fuzzy is an invitation to nights of teeth-grinding and premature gray hair.

Let me illustrate "fuzzy" with a case study.

Let's say you are called to a congregation where the music director has been there twenty-two years. She is both an employee of the church and a member of the congregation. Right off the bat, there is potential role confusion for her and for you. Is she mainly a

Part Four: Tough Stuff

church employee or mostly a church member? Are you her pastor or are you her supervisor/employer?

I am not saying never hire church members. But both employee and employer need to think twice and try to anticipate some of the potential challenges.

But back to our case study and music director...

The choir members, all seven of them, with an average age of sixty-nine, love the music director. But she appears to have stopped adding anything to her repertoire sometime in the previous millennium. Should you make a suggestion she has an amazing ability to give you the impression she has heard you, gets it, and will follow through and yet... nothing happens. Not a blessed thing.

Meanwhile, the "by-laws" of the church, indicate that you as the minister are her "supervisor." However, the music committee does her annual evaluation and recommends compensation to the board. The music director herself believes—though there is no evidence to support it—that she was "called" by the congregation and is really accountable to them—not you. She thinks you are a "wonderful young person," with good intentions, but she understands the congregation (far better than you do).

I wish this were a parody. Alas...

It is not unusual that the personnel "system" of a congregation is a swamp of confusion, with an alligator or two lurking under the surface. Those who benefit from the general murkiness, or are simply oblivious to it, may say, "Well, gosh, it has worked okay until now" (i.e., until you came). Don't bet on it.

So, if you find yourself considering a position as a lead pastor or a solo pastor—and before you say "yes" and sign on that dotted line—ask to look at the church by-laws and personnel policy.

If those documents indicate the person in the position you are considering is the "supervisor" for other staff, ask what that means and how it works. Ask who does evaluations for staff members. What are the discipline and grievance procedures, and who implements them? Who has hire/fire power? Raise questions. Ask for clarification. Ask how this has been working for them. Have they had conflicts in relation to staff or personnel issues?

If a congregation has a document that locates these powers and responsibilities with another group, e.g. a personnel committee, that may be fine—if they do their job. Ask about that. But if the documents say that the minister has those responsibilities, probe to see if that is for real. When you meet with those on the staff gently explore how they see these things.

So, the larger point is, if you are working in a church personnel system that is fuzzy, a system where personal relationships—the music director's brother chairs the board of trustees, and their family have been members since before Jesus was born are what counts—proceed with caution.

If there is clarity about who's on first and people aren't, by and large, wearing multiple hats, thank God and your lucky stars!

Go in with eyes as open as you can manage. If the system is fuzzy, informal, and boundaries are a mess, you will want to work on that and try over time to move the needle from "confusion" toward "clarity." That is a long-term piece of work. Changing this system is not something to try to do in year one, unless you have a clear mandate to do so. Normally, you've got to build up some credit and trust.

This letter may raise for you the whole hoary specter of "church administration." Many clergy bemoan "administrative" work and say they never signed on for it in the first place. Their concerns are "spiritual." To me that smells of the ancient heresy of "docetism," with its sharp separation of the "spiritual" and "material."

The administrative stuff can, yes, be a pain in the butt. But it can also be thought of as pastoral care. When the workings of a church, including personnel stuff, are reasonably clear and reliable, it creates trust. The converse is also true.

If you are head of staff, you don't have to do all the administrative work yourself (and you shouldn't), but you do need to make sure it does get done and done reasonably well by someone.

Sending love . . .

Bullies

Dear Ones,

Bullies in the church? How is that possible? Aren't people in the church nice people, caring people?

On his first day on the job Jesus ran into a man with "an unclean spirit" (Mark 1:21–28). Note where Jesus encountered this demonic power. Inside the synagogue, which by analogy, is like inside the church. What better place to be up to no good than where people are kind of assumed to be doing good?

Now, all of us behave badly at times, when stressed, frightened, hurt, or overwhelmed. But this isn't what we're talking about. Nor are we talking about someone who is a critic.

Being a bully is of a different order of magnitude. A bully is someone who is willing to destroy you, other people, or the church. They aren't just difficult or prickly. They are malicious. And also clever. They can be charming one day or in one setting, but awful the next or in another setting.

And, in my experience, they have never done anything wrong. At least that's the way they see it. Everything wrong in the world is somebody else's fault. Usually yours. Never theirs.

So, yes there can be bullies in the church, but be cautious about using the label. The term *bully* should not be used casually or easily. But in some cases it does fit.

How does a church deal with a bully?

Well, for openers, you don't wait until you got one in front of you frothing at the mouth. Work to create a healthy congregation because a healthy body is one with a strong immune system that can fight off viruses and malignancies. (Remember Paul is all about the church as the body of Christ and building up the body.)

Books have been written about healthy congregations—not my task here. But I would just mention a couple of things that seem to me kind of crucial.

It's good to think about, talk about, and have norms for appropriate (and inappropriate) behavior. Think of your family. When we have problems with each other there are some ways we handle that, while some behaviors that are pretty much off the table. Schools do that. Churches can do that too. Norms may be drawn from Scripture, from a congregation's history and traditions, or from secular sources of insight.

An example of a norm might be, "If you have a complaint or some kind of charge to lodge, you put your name on it and we will deal with it." So, the corollary norm is, "We don't send nasty, anonymous letters and when we get them we don't respond (I mean, how could we?)."

Another general observation I'd make about healthy congregations and pastors is that they face hard stuff rather than sweeping it under the rug or pretending everything is peachy-keen when it isn't. Rabbi Edwin Friedman,[9] a great writer on these topics, says that, "every dysfunctional congregation is headed by a peace-monger," that is someone who will do anything to avoid conflict or confrontation. I'm not saying you have to go to the mat over everything. But you can't avoid real issues.

There's tons more to say on this topic, but the important point for now is that a healthy body can fight off infection. Same with a congregation. The first line of defense is to strengthen the body.

In my experience bullies focus almost totally on themselves. What doesn't seem to register is, as a wise friend put it, "the group (i.e. the congregation) has a life too."

But what if prevention doesn't work and you have a bully?

- First, get a reality check. Consult with trusted others/experts. Is this what I think it is? Am I over-reacting? Under-reacting?

---

9. Friedman, *A Failure of Nerve*, 13.

PART FOUR: TOUGH STUFF

- Second, document stuff: meetings, outbursts, stuff that just seems weird.
- Third, do not talk yourself into thinking that if only I/we are nicer or more understanding he or she will change, come around. He/she will not come around.
- Fourth, don't let a bully's attacks or narrative go unanswered. Ask your leadership team and key people of influence to help to get an accurate story out.
- Fifth, while responding to attacks and misinformation, do not stoop to a bully's level, i.e. personal attacks, sending angry emails via "Reply All," or by being provoked to reactive behaviors you will later regret.
- Sixth, never meet with such a person alone (to do so allows them to deliberately misunderstand or misquote you).
- Seventh, be very careful with any written communications to a bully. Don't put anything in writing that you aren't prepared to see posted online for all the world to see.
- Eighth, don't play their game, meaning don't attend meetings they set up or let them create the process or choose the mediator.
- Nine, do not think they will simply go away.
- And, ten, be prepared to terminate a bully's membership in the church.[10]

Okay, that's a heavy list on a heavy topic, perhaps not quite letter material. And I hope you never have to use it (except for the preventive, strengthen-the-immune-system part).

Last thought, possibly repetitive, someone acting in bullying ways does not mean you are a bad minister. It might mean just the opposite. "When the Word of God is alive," said Martin Luther, "evil spirits are set in motion." Which takes us back to my beginning: Jesus bringing the reign of God cranked up the evil spirits.

Sending love . . .

---

10. I am indebted to Michael Piazza and his workshop on "Dealing with Bullies" for the Center for Progressive Renewal.

The Former Pastor Problem

Dear Ones,

Dating myself (though I guess I've managed that already), Joni Mitchell's song "Both Sides Now" comes to mind.

I have seen this one from both sides. I've been a pastor who had my predecessor(s) in the congregation and community. And I've been a former pastor who tries to negotiate a healthy relationship with congregations I once served and the clergy who serve them now.

Beyond that, in my time as a congregational consultant, I was impressed (or was it "depressed?") by just how frequently problems in churches nestled around a former minister who seemed to have totally forgotten everything she or he once knew about boundaries. There are way too many such stories.

There are reasons for that. The relationship between a pastor and a congregation is unlike any other. It is intimate. You share the toughest and the most joyful times in the lives of those you shepherd. They become accustomed, through your preaching and teaching, to regularly interpreting life with you and often through your eyes. You each come to occupy a lot of psychic space in each other's heart and soul.

One sign of how deep this relationship is just how peculiar it is when it ends. One day your whole life is bound up with a particular community of people. A day later, on resignation or retirement, that is over and done—and there's no going back. If not literally true, it is certainly true figuratively. It's a kind of death. And it hurts.

Even if, as a pastor, you know you are ready for change and have prepared for it, there's nothing quite so strange as this one, at least in my experience.

How pastors and congregations handle this death varies depending on lots of factors. One is the norms in your denomination. Some denominations are quite clear and prescriptive: a former minister shall not continue as a member or active participant in a congregation they once served. Period. The End.

That may seem draconian, but there's a reason for it. In order for a congregation to "fall in love" with their new pastor, they have to an open place in their hearts. They have to be, in the language of folks who study relationships, "emotionally available."

In many denominations, though, the guidance on all this is far more ambiguous. It is left up to the former pastor, the new pastor, and the congregation's leaders to sort out.

If a former pastor does continue to participate in a congregation they once served, they really have to have terrific boundaries. Why? Because the littlest things—an arched eyebrow, a muttered aside, a roll of the eyes—can communicate reservation or disapproval.

Of course, some former pastors go well beyond that. They agree to preside at funerals or weddings (without consulting their successor). They want to lead a Bible study or other group experience with church members. Worse, they are active behind the scenes players in the dramas of congregational life. Sometimes a spouse or close friends serve as their proxies.

Oh Lord, GET A LIFE!

What I've noticed when these kinds of things happen is that the former minister believes him or herself to be a special case. They know that playing such roles is problematic or unethical in the abstract, but somehow they just don't think the rules were meant to apply to them. They are different. Special.

Sorry, no.

But who communicates that and keeps folks accountable? It can be the new pastor, but that's asking a lot of someone who is just building trust. Better if it comes from able lay leaders or judicatory officials who understand the issues, care about the former pastor,

THE FORMER PASTOR PROBLEM

but who are able to be very clear with that person. "You are no longer the pastor; don't act like it, don't meddle."

Some congregations and former pastors pull this new relationship off well. Many don't. When it does work, it can be a valuable—even beautiful—thing, a witness to everyone involved of continuity and respect.

If former pastors need to be very circumspect and mind their boundaries, congregations not only need to do the same, but something more: extend some honor and acknowledgment to a former pastor and their family. That may take the form of asking that person to preach or assist in serving communion once a year (say on All Saints, Thanksgiving Sunday, or Memorial Day), or to participate in occasions that celebrate the congregation's history. Don't simply neglect the former pastor or turn him or her into a pariah. They deserve respect and acknowledgment of their service. Including, gracefully, can humanize. Excluding can make a former pastor larger than life.

In the best possible world, an outgoing pastor and congregation will discuss and clarify their expectations of one another for the future prior to the conclusion of the pastoral covenant. And they will ritualize the end of that covenant in congregational worship. There are services for that in many worship books.

So, here's the executive summary: if you have a predecessor who remains a part of the congregation and you have concerns about their boundaries/behavior, don't let that go on unaddressed. All too often, it only gets worse.

But on the other hand, if you have a predecessor who remains part of the congregation and exhibits good boundaries, treat that person with respect and affection and help your congregation to do the same. It can be a source of strength for everyone concerned.

Shortly after I left the last congregation I served I ran into a retired conference minister as I did a guest preacher/teacher stint. He said to me, "How do you like being a ghost?" His bittersweet description of the reality of being a "former pastor." You show up one Sunday after having not been around for three years and people may look as if they've seen a ghost.

Part Four: Tough Stuff

But it is best when neither a congregation nor a pastor are haunted by the past. Exorcisms require attention and intentionality on the part of both former pastor and congregation. It is worth the investment of time and energy.

Sending love . . .

Money

Dear Ones,

People are funny about money.

Our feelings about money are complex, deep-seated, and often defy reason or logic. So it's no wonder that it's not uncommon to hear someone who is new to a congregation say, "I'll do anything to help out—just don't make me ask people for money."

A fair number of young clergy probably feel that same way. I pretty much did. But among other things that happened at my first church was that the congregation voted to have a capital drive to add on to the building.

With that on the agenda, there was no place to hide. I had to think about money and talk about money. My family and I had to make decisions about money and giving.

Here's my testimony: I am grateful that I had to address the topic head-on. Therapists will tell you that the stuff you really don't want to talk about is exactly the stuff you do need to talk about. That goes for congregations too. Many congregations shroud the topic of money in secrecy and anxiety. By doing so we almost always give it a lot more power than it deserves.

Maybe that's why money was a topic Jesus talked about a lot. Second only to the kingdom of God, it turns out. And that continues in Acts and in the letters of the New Testament. If you take the Scriptures seriously, not talking about money requires some pretty fancy dancing.

As I said, I'm grateful that the church, and a capital fund drive, gave me a push to face into the topic.

Part Four: Tough Stuff

Really, that's job #1 here—deal with your own stuff around money. The first (but never completely finished step) for clergy who are going to talk with a congregation about money is to face and work through your own feelings and hang-ups on the topic. A fair number of clergy are judgy and not a little self-righteous about money and people who have it. If you don't do your own work first those kinds of feelings tend to come out in not very productive ways like resentment or guilt-tripping.

So, start by processing your own feelings and values around money.

I learned not long ago that I am a "five" on the Enneagram, "an investigator." I like to learn stuff, to figure things out, to observe and analyze and to find patterns and connections. These were qualities that were helpful as a pastor. They also made me a good church consultant.

But every type on the Enneagram has a shadow, a besetting sin. For us five's it is avarice. That doesn't necessarily mean that we're into accumulation or possessions. It does mean we worry that there won't be enough, that we will run out.

My upbringing around money, by two Depression-era parents, dovetailed pretty well with that. Making money and saving money (I had my first job delivering papers at age eight; my first savings account at age nine) was definitely encouraged. Spending not so much.

So, I had to come to grips with all that, which has proven to be a very good thing. Thanks to the church, I have learned to be far more generous and far less anxious. For that I am truly grateful. I've come to enjoy giving money away—which it turns out is the only way to have enough. Bit of a gospel paradox, that.

But after, or as, you work through your own stuff about money, you get the opportunity to help others do the same. And the point is not mainly about meeting the annual budget or success in a capital fund drive, although both are nice. The point is faith, faithfulness, and living what Jesus called an "abundant life," which is more about loving lots than having lots.

People, including clergy, tend to groan when "stewardship season" rolls around. We boil it down to "asking for money," and as noted above, a lot of people would paint the entire fellowship hall or run a marathon rather than ask for money. (That said, there is a time for the respectful "ask." You'd be amazed how often people respond generously to a clear request.)

Nevertheless, my point is that by talking about money, we are often pretty close to the basics: our fears and our faith. Learning, as I did, a practice of greater generosity can be transforming. And that's really the business we're in as churches, the transformation of people's lives by the grace of God.

One of things you'll want to do in the first year of a new ministry is try to figure out what the congregation's "culture" is around money. Is it fairly open? Or deeply secretive? Is there comfort in talking about money? Or does the anxiety go way up when the topic is mentioned? Who has power around money, and who does not? A congregation's "culture" around money and understanding of it will tell you a lot.

One particular issue that will probably come up is this. Do you, as the minister, know what people give to the church? There are good arguments on both sides. If the culture of a congregation is strongly set against the minister knowing what people give, you probably don't want to take that head-on right away.

But I've usually been in the loop, that is, knowing what people give. Provided you treat such information respectfully and don't blab about it in the wrong places and to the wrong people, knowing something about people's giving and patterns of giving has pastoral value. When there's a significant change in someone's pattern of giving that is important information. It may tell you that something is going on in that person's or family's life. Or they may be concerned about something the church is doing or not doing. It may alert you too to a potential for growth and change.

Also, many congregations that don't talk about money are often reliant on a small number of big givers. Who may be getting on in years. You kind of need to be clued in on that bit of reality.

Part Four: Tough Stuff

There's a lot more to be said on this topic. I say some of it in my little book *Stewardship for Vital Congregations*.[11]

For now, suffice it to say that money and how we use it is a kind of barometer of our faith and spiritual health. Just as going sailing without checking the barometer would be not smart, so ignoring the role of money in people's lives and in the life of the church is a missed opportunity.

Sending love . . .

---

11. Robinson, *Stewardship for Vital Congregations*.

PART FIVE

The Future of the Church

Dealing with the Narrative of Decline

Dear Ones,

As Dickens famously wrote in *A Tale of Two Cities*, "It was the best of times; it was the worst of times."

Which is it as you enter the ministry in the first quarter of the twenty-first century? I could argue either one. That is, that you are on the edge of the new thing God is doing, or you are at the tail end of mainline Protestantism's downward spiral.

As I began my ministry, forty years ago, mainline Protestant churches had already been losing members and churches for at least a decade. But mostly we in the mainline Protestant world were loath to see the handwriting on the wall.

My first church was in a small town about thirty miles outside of Seattle. We stood proudly on Main Street, across from the town library, kitty-cornered from the elementary school, and a few doors from town hall. That was the civic establishment and we were part of it. Less so, the Catholic church in town, which was down a side street. And then there were a couple of storefront churches, one Baptist, one Pentecostal. We were clearly the establishment.

But appearances can be deceiving. Though we were a quite moderate congregation by UCC standards, we were somewhere out on the left flank of that town's sociologically and theologically.

Which might not have been a problem, if we didn't so fervently believe that we were the "mainline," and the place where all right-thinking people and families would find themselves in due course. To put it bluntly, we assumed that we had a "guaranteed market share," even as the religious world was becoming both more fragmented and competitive.

Much of my ministry has been shaped by that early experience and my awareness that a mainline congregation such as ours, for all its strengths, was losing touch with large segments of the culture. Even as our society became more fragmented and secular, we assumed our place and privilege.

Fast forward to the present. Now the mainline Protestant church has been in institutional decline for fifty years, and everyone is, if belatedly, onto it.

The "narrative of decline" has been chronicled in newspapers and television specials, highlighted in research studies, and lamented in seminaries. But in many churches you don't need a research study. Just look around. Folks are old. If your youth group is people in their sixties, well, you have a problem.

Not everywhere. But many places.

If we were in denial about any problem or challenge forty years ago now the pendulum has swung. Swung from denial to what feels like resignation. From bravado to fatalism. Forty years ago, it was, "What, me worry?" Now, there's a bit of, "Abandon hope all ye who enter here."

Both are wrong. Denial of change and challenge is a big problem. But perhaps even more problematic is the conclusion of many churches that decline unto death is inevitable.

At least sometimes, as the resurrection stories tell us, we adjust to death. Our real fear is of life. Churches too can fear life. These days some churches are accepting decline, even death, because life is too scary.

It is, at any rate, clear that the mainline Protestant churches are no longer culturally dominant, no longer the "default religious option" in American society. But that doesn't mean we don't have a role to play and a gift to give.

Here's a thought experiment/analogy.

Back in the day there were "Mom and Pop" grocery stores on the corner in many neighborhoods. Given your age, you may never have seen one, but trust me, they did exist. Many of our churches were sort of like the Mom and Pop stores. Part of the community. A little funky. Close to home. Not especially fancy. Limited choices. In addition to the Mom and Pops, we had some larger, usually city-center churches that were sort of like a Safeway store. Bigger, brighter, more to choose from.

Then along came Costco and Walmart, which for the church world was the megachurch. Easy access, low prices, lots of choices.

Where does that leave us? Where we live we have member-owned Puget Consumer Co-ops (PCC). Once a hippie thing, co-op groceries—at least this one—has evolved. They are pretty snappy, high-quality, healthy, and organic. They welcome all, but they aren't for everybody. Still, they have a real place in the overall scene.

I wonder if we can find some hints for our future in these co-op stores? Friendly, high quality, local, and participatory. Not a Costco or Walmart, but not a dusty, run-down Mom and Pop either . . . as I say, a thought-experiment . . . Could we liberal or progressive or mainline churches be analogous to the co-op niche in grocery stores? Maybe not the biggest church in town, but great quality and part of the community?

But let's come at this business of a "narrative of decline" from a different, more theological, angle.

If I read the biblical story at all accurately, it seems to me that God sort of specializes in situations of decline and people who might be said to be unlikely choices or in one state of decline or another.

Think Abraham and Sarah. Well into their declining years, God shows up to announce that these two childless old crocs will become mother and father of a new people, a people as numerous as the grains of sand on the seashore. Sarah finds this hilarious, though perhaps in a "you have got to be kidding" sort of way.

Then as if to make it perfectly clear, God stalls on fulfilling the promise for another several decades, at which point Abraham and Sarah were, as Paul later wrote, "as good as dead." Only then, is a child, Issac, born. "Issac" means laughter. Get it? This is a God thing. It is not about Abraham and Sarah's incredible strength or their human potential. Because, well, they had none.

89

Part Five: The Future of the Church

It is about grace. It is about God's capacity to do a new, an unexpected thing. It is about God's capacity to "give life to the dead and call into existence the things that do not exist" (Romans 4:17).

The real antidote to the narrative of decline is the biblical narrative. Who knows, our "decline" could be a blessing in disguise, calling us back to raw, naked basics—the power and grace of God—so that we may go forward?

When we are in touch with this story, the story of God's improbable, impossible grace, even "the worst of times" become something else altogether. They become "the best of times."

Sending love...

How Do We Breathe Life into the Institutional Church?

Dear Ones,

This is a great question you've asked, one that a lot of clergy and laity are asking in one way or another these days. Sometimes it just seems that the weight of the institution is as burdensome and overwhelming as Saul's armor was for young David.

Two quick responses to the question as you've framed it. Then a longer reflection on how renewal happens in churches.

First, "how do we breathe life into the institutional church?" Answer: we don't. God does. For sure, we have a role to play. We can be instruments of God's resurrection power. But it's not all up to us. If we think it is all on us, it will crush us.

Second, the phrase "institutional church" might suggest there is a church somewhere that is not an institution. I'm not sure that's true. Any human group that organizes itself at all for some sort of purpose is a kind of institution. The problem is not institutions per se. It is whether or not our institutions have a capacity for renewal.

My guess is that one of the reasons so many people today despair of "the institutional church" is that many of these institutions aren't showing much capacity for or receptivity toward renewal. They appear to be repeating the slogans of yesterday that don't address the challenges of the today, let alone the future.

I've been working, as have many, at church renewal for a long time now. If I had "the" answer about how renewal happens or a

Part Five: The Future of the Church

surefire, foolproof method or technique, I'd have sold many more books and be much wealthier than I am!

There isn't any one answer or strategy for bringing life-giving breath, a.k.a. the Holy Spirit, to fill our churches. But here are my thoughts.

One thing I notice in many churches that might be described as "stuck" is that the church itself has become the primary focus. What do I mean by that? When "our church" has become the focus you are likely to hear people talking a lot about their particular church and how wonderful (great/ important/ unique/special) it is. Or the self-talk may be negative: our church is too old, too small, too (fill in the blank). But instead of being expansive and confident, there's an inward focus.

To be clear, having a sense of the story and beauty of a particular congregation can be a fine thing. I guess what I'm talking about is confusing our church with God. Thinking it is all about "our community," or "our uniqueness." We are not a satisfactory substitute for God.

There's a story about an old priest who wanders into church and sees a banner that reads, "God Is Other People." The priest takes a marker and makes a change so that the banner now reads, "God Is Other, People." Community and other people are very important, but the priest's editing also had a point.

A subtle aspect of this focus on us is that, at least often, it tends to be accompanied by a division or boundary between insiders and outsiders, longtime members and newcomers. People may deny this, but churches that focus on themselves overly much tend to become clubs, with definite in and out groups that belie the truth and promise of the gospel.

It is inevitable that there is some of this in every church (or other human group/organization). Part of fallen human nature.

But what I notice about churches where there is greater vitality is that the focus is less on the church itself and more on God (Jesus, Holy Spirit). In such churches the church is not an end in itself, but a means to a larger end. The church has a sense of purpose or mission bigger than its own survival. It has a lively sense that God has called it to this venture and that God is with them in it.

How Do We Breathe Life into the Institutional Church?

You may remember a story I told in my sermon at your ordination, Laura. It was about a dying church in a major city in the southeast. Historically the church had served a German ethnic population from its massive, fortress-like stone structure covering a downtown block. It had been, in its day, "a great church." But change, as it does, happened. The onetime German-American community around the church became increasingly African American. The German-American members had aged and become a small, inwardly focused enclave worried about their survival.

Though the story is longer and more complicated, a new minister was called who was an African American woman. With her help, the congregation began to connect anew with the community in which they were set as well as to rediscover the power of faith. The church began to experience new life and growth.

When I was in town to speak at a conference, I met this pastor. I told her that I heard something about the story of this church and of her ministry there. I said I would love to visit. She said, "We'd love to have you." Then she added, "Yes, come and see what God is doing!"

Do you hear where the focus is? It's not so much about us and our special church. It is about God. "Come and see what God is doing." It is about God's renewing, healing, liberating, and transforming work in people's lives and in the world. And it is about us participating in God's mission in the world.

When the pastor has such a faith and focus, and when some others in leadership share it, then renewal becomes possible, even likely.

I would add just a bit more about how you get to that focus on God (Jesus, Holy Spirit) instead of being overly focused on us and how wonderful or not wonderful we are.

Dive into Scripture. Take it seriously. In the Bible, it is God who is the acting subject of the story. The Bible is really God's story. Learn that story, love that story, preach that story. That will tend to get you focused more on God and less on us and will tend to call us out of ourselves.

Focus on Jesus. He is amazing. Always upsetting expectations. Forever turning the world upside down.

Part Five: The Future of the Church

Put your best into worship, making it God focused and centered.

But be warned. If a church has devolved over some years into some kind of club with insiders and outsiders, the insiders won't be thrilled about this focus because well, it's not about them and will challenge the system of privilege they have created. Such preaching, teaching, and worship almost inevitably calls into question insider power. This is where being "wise as serpents and gentle as doves" (Matthew 10:16), to quote Jesus, comes in.

If God, the God of Sarah and Abraham, Moses and Miriam, Mary and Paul is alive in the midst of the congregation and God's redeeming work in this world is our focus, then the church will be alive.

There's no magic. Except that ... this actually is sort of magic.

Sending love ...

PART SIX

The Church of the Future

Building the Front Porch

DEAR ONES,

When I was a kid, in the previous century, the church and particularly the mainline Protestant churches enjoyed a lot of support from the surrounding American culture.

Not the least of it was a fairly strong sense of expectation that people would be part of a church (or synagogue). The question then was not so much whether to be a part of church or not, but which one?

There were many other ways in which church and society were woven together in a reciprocal relationship. A big one, where I grew up, was that all stores were closed on Sunday. In fact, there wasn't a whole lot else going on Sundays except church.

I could go on enumerating the ways the church was supported by the surrounding culture and that mainline Protestant bodies enjoyed a "most favored church" status within the spectrum.

But the real point is that things have changed. A lot. The church is no longer so supported by the surrounding culture, its norms and practices.

That said, there's a lot of regional variation to this. In the southeast and Midwest, churches continue to enjoy some support from the culture. But in many places the surrounding culture is pretty much indifferent to the church, while in some there is suspicion, even negativity. The northwest, where I live, is somewhere between indifferent and negative. We've been known for a while as "the None Zone," because census data indicates such a large number of people respond "none" to a question about religious affiliation.

Part Six: The Church of the Future

One might bemoan and complain about these changes. A better response is to note the changes, face into the new reality, and adapt.

That seems to me the big challenge facing leaders like you—helping faith communities adapt to a different world and to do so creatively and faithfully.

In this letter, I want to highlight three strategies that seem to me exciting adaptive responses. These three each have fancy names, but we will unpack them. The three are recovering the catechumenate, being a missional church, and what I have dubbed "front-porch ministries." Each one tries to build new points of connection between a church and the community in which it is set.

Here, just a brief exploration of three ways churches are discovering new life and engagement and having some fun doing it.

The catechumenate is a fancy word for the process used in the ancient church to prepare people to be baptized and become a part of the church. When Christianity wasn't the religion of the society, but an alternative, baptism was a big deal.

Today, baptism itself, and how it is changing, is revealing. In the previous era, baptism of children was something "you did" as good parents. In the course of my ministry there has been, however, a big shift. Now, not all baptisms are of infants or children. Increasingly, it is adults, often young adults, who we baptize. These folks have come to faith and church for the first time as adults.

I think that is incredibly exciting.

But how does a church welcome and support those who are new to the whole thing, who want to explore this faith perhaps for the first time, and discover what it's about? Some churches are creating a "twenty-first century" version of the ancient catechumenate, an experience through which inquirers or seekers can ask questions, build relationships, learn a way of life.

The contemporary versions of the catechumenate I like best tend to use small groups for people to ask questions, share experiences, and journey toward the font and the transformation of life it represents. Because such small groups usually pair a seeker with a mentor who is a member of the church, this is a "two-for." Both the newcomers and the people who've been around a while, and now shepherd others, grow in faith and relationship. There is lots more

BUILDING THE FRONT PORCH

to be said about the work being done around a catechumenate for the twenty-first century. And there are books, articles, and videos out there to learn more.[12]

The main point is that you don't assume everyone who lives in your town is already Christian and all they need to do is get their butt in the pew. You create safe ways for people to come in and for that to be really transformative and healing (for both the seeker and the community of faith).

If the catechumenate builds a ramp, so to speak, into the church, the missional church approach goes the other direction, from inside out.

While the term *missional church* can mean many different things, for our purposes here it comes down to getting to know your community, building relationships, and being committed to your neighborhood, however you define the 'hood.

This pretty much starts with learning and listening. What's going on in the neighborhood? Who lives here? What are their stories and challenges? You go hang out where people are, coffee shops, brew pubs, schools. You identify people to get to know and to learn from, say the mayor, a cop, a realtor, a school guidance counselor, a community activist.

And as you are learning, you are asking yourself, "What is God already up to here in this community, this neighborhood?" And you ask, "If God's mission is, as our Jewish sisters and brothers say, mending the world, how is that happening here and how can we be part of it?"

So, if the catechumenate builds a metaphorical ramp into the life of the congregation, and missional church builds a ramp or bridge out, "front-porch" ministries land somewhere in between.

I got this idea when we lived for a year in Toronto. In an older section of the city where we lived each home had a front porch. Often in the evenings we would go for a walk and frequently we chatted with people who sat on their front porch.

---

12. Hoffman, *Faith Forming Faith* and *Faith Shaping Ministry*, are two I recommend.

Part Six: The Church of the Future

The front porch was an in-between space. Not quite public, but neither was it private. It was in between outside and inside, and as such a place for interaction between the two.

Here are a couple of examples of churches that have built a front-porch ministry. One church hosts a farmer's market in its parking lot once a week. In the midst of the market, the church has a table and chairs, coffee, water, and lemonade. People are welcome to sit, have a drink and a chat. Relationships are formed. Information about the church is available.

Or another church operates a coffee house. And another a brew pub. They host discussions of various books and topics. They are places to interact, practice hospitality, build relationships that don't involve walking in the door of the church, but sitting on or standing by the front porch.

Still another church has a used clothing store, where items can be free if that's what's needed, in a store front downtown. Some other churches create a church/community garden as another sort of front porch.

Whether it's helping people come in (the catechumenate) or go out (missional church) or find a middle ground between the two (front porch) the idea is adapting to our new situation means being intentional about building relationships and connections.

Remember, our God doesn't sit at home waiting for us to show up. This God takes the initiative, who comes out seeking us and welcomes us with great joy.

Sending love . . .

Telling the Truth

Dear Ones,

In my last letter, I said that a seismic shift that has been unfolding over several decades now. The churches, most especially the mainline Protestant churches, have been disestablished. Mostly, we do not enjoy the social supports we once did.

While it is true that in North America the church was never established in the ways it was in Europe, for example, being tax-supported (Lutheran Churches in Scandinavia and Germany) or being known as the state church, e.g., the Church of England, and integrated into the rituals of the monarchy and governance, nevertheless . . . mainline Protestant churches did enjoy a kind of "unofficial" establishment status. We were the church "on the town green." We were considered a civic institution and often as part of the leadership of a town or community.

As such, we got used to counting on the culture to do Christian formation with and for us. That was the "no shopping on Sundays" thing and a whole lot more, e.g., Christmas programs in the public schools, no school on Good Friday, etc. With that largely over, we need to discover new ways to connect, to ways to form people in the Christian faith and life. It's actually a wonderful opportunity and challenge.

There was another implication of our quasi-establishment status. It showed up in funny ways, like, "The pastor is coming to visit. Put away your beer bottle." Or, "Good Christians don't swear," or "Good Christians are supposed to have kids who get straight A's, letter in sports, and never use drugs, get arrested, or get in trouble."

Part Six: The Church of the Future

In other words, being a "good Christian" meant that you were a really good, above average, outstanding sort of person.

There are a couple of problems with this. One is that it's the old "works righteousness" trap. The implicit but strong message was this, "If you are really, really good—basically perfect—then God will love you." It is what some call "a religion of virtue." The virtuous are loved, saved, and acceptable to God, to other people, and to themselves.

But that's not the gospel. The gospel is that, sinner that you are, God loves you and is for you. Dietrich Bonhoeffer put it this way, "It is the grace of the gospel, which is so hard for the pious to understand, that it confronts us with the truth and says: You are a sinner, a great, desperate sinner; come now, as the sinner that you are, to God who loves you. He wants you as you are; he does not want anything from you, a sacrifice, a work; he wants you alone."[13]

When we get the idea that Christians are the good people, a kind of moral elite, and that Christianity is really a religion of virtue and for the virtuous, another problem is that it invites a kind of dishonesty. After all, if screwing up will mean that God doesn't love you and that you don't belong among God's people, then who would ever admit to screwing up?

So, churches during our establishment era often became places where people pretended. Pretended that they had it all together. Pretended that they had no problems more serious than maybe being late occasionally, or sometimes indulging in too many chips or too much chocolate.

Just the other day, I spoke with a clergy friend who was thinking back on a previous pastorate and when things began to go wrong. "It was when I covered up that my daughter had an addiction." To admit this to others in the church would have made her feel she failed as a Christian and a pastor.

But this game of pretend had another effect. It tended to create a culture that made it hard to tell the truth. We gave off subtle, and

---

13. Bonhoeffer, *Life Together*, 111.

sometimes less than subtle signals that "shut down honest expressions of pain, vulnerability and disclosure."[14]

A group like AA, where people did tell the truth about their fuckups, generally ended up in the church basement because such truth telling didn't have a place upstairs in the sanctuary.

We had, in our own way, a lot in common with the Pharisees who Jesus was always bumping up against. They were very earnest folks who worked very hard to fulfill the law's every requirement and to be totally virtuous.

They, the Pharisees, were suspicious of the company Jesus kept. They thought he ate with the wrong people—prostitutes, low-level cons (a.k.a. "tax collectors), and other ne'er-do-wells. When they voiced their concern, he said, "I did not come for the healthy but for the sick." Thing is, from Jesus' point of view we're all sick, broken, lost, and in need of grace and mercy.

This has been a kind of long run-up, to say this: the church of the future will be a place where we can tell the truth, where we can be real about who we are, how we too have screwed up, and our need for help.

The idea is not, however, to wallow in our failures and foibles, but to face them as part of a process of healing and transformation.

Some of this starts with us as pastors. When I was a young pastor I thought, without thinking about it too much, that I needed to be more or less perfect. Like my aforementioned colleague. I imagined my job was to be the most spiritual, most caring, best Christian in the crowd. This was, of course, a load of crap. Moreover, it's a really heavy, truly a crushing, load to carry.

As time and life went on I realized that I too had my own stuff, that I was in Bonhoeffer's words, "a great, desperate sinner." I also came to suspect that I would be more helpful as a pastor if I owned up to my own pride, blindness, arrogance, and need for grace.

That said, I find that some contemporary preachers go to the opposite extreme, recounting their flops and foibles as if they were merit badges. Not only does it get tiresome to listen to a preacher

14. Baskette, *Standing Naked*, 11.

who talks too much about her or himself, we're not the real focus here—God is.

So, our truth-telling should be thoughtful and deliberate, and not another—if upside-down—form of spiritual boasting.

Beyond what we communicate in our sermons and self-understanding, I'm intrigued by congregations that have been trying to create a community where truth-telling is possible. Many have learned a lot about this from AA, or another recovery group, in the basement.

Consider one such congregation in Somerville, Massachusetts. It's reframing of the traditional confession of sin in worship is told by our colleague, Molly Baskette, in her book, *Standing Naked: The Art of Public Confession Before God*.

The richness of her account resists easy summation, so I encourage you to read it for yourselves. But I will say this: it's a practice that can be adopted and adapted by, as Molly says, "any church in America."

Members of the congregation invite people to bring their own stories of sin, struggle, and failure before God and the congregation. Pastors work carefully to prepare people and to create a climate in which it is safe to be honest and vulnerable. Members of the congregations might confess things like lying, being annoying neat freaks, discovering just how angry they can be with their own kids, or avoiding people in distress.

Even if we don't dive full bore into what that particular church has done, there are other ways to encourage telling the truth. Often congregations find that small groups are a place where people can be encouraged to safely tell the truth about our lives and so permit God to move among us.

Yet another congregation has taken cues from the National Public Radio program "The Moth." This church in Chicago, Gilead, builds its services around a theme from Scripture, inviting people to both hear stories and share their own. The intent is to create a safe setting in which to tell the truth and be vulnerable and explore where and how God may be at work.

You might say that this whole venture in truth-telling is a kind of "recovery" movement or for the church. Instead of seeing ourselves as those who are "better than others," we try to see ourselves as people who also stand in need of grace, and to join with others who are committed to the work of transformation and healing.

The bottom line here is really a theological one. I like the aphorism (I'm not sure whose it is), "Salvation is all about grace; ethics is all about gratitude." That is, salvation is God's work of grace in us. It is a gift. Our efforts at living lives of faith, hope, and love are our expression of gratitude for God's grace—not an attempt to win or deserve it.

Sending love . . .

Pay Attention to the Energy

DEAR ONES,

This letter is about worship and leading worship.

During the years of my ministry, worship has been the focus of all kinds of debate and experimentation, renewal and reform. A lot of this debate has revolved around music and some version of traditional vs. contemporary music and worship styles. Sometimes things got so hot people called it "the Worship Wars."

What I note about most of this controversy is that it is a kind of head trip. That is, the debates are about categories like "right and wrong," "correct and incorrect," or "what I like and what I don't like." You can hear that a lot of this involves and gets us into what might be called our judging selves.

But worship, when it's alive and faithful, tends to get us out of our heads alone and move us into our hearts. It somehow sidesteps that part of us that is busy making judgments and invites us to a different and deeper consciousness.

A UCC colleague of ours, Janice Springer, in a brilliant but little-known book, *Nurturing Spiritual Depth in Christian Worship*, offers a different approach altogether. She urges that we "consider what happens to the energy."

It's important to say right away that by "energy" Springer is not primarily speaking about our own energy. Nor is she talking about emotions or whether worship leaders are energetic or somehow amped up. The energy of which she speaks is God's.

She writes, "Worship can be—I would say it *should* be—about power. It is about God's power. It is about how to access that power for our lives, for our service to others, for our justice-making. It is about how not to abuse power. Because power is energy, I have learned to pay attention to energy in worship. I notice that if I fail to do so, most of us will not get out of our heads."[15]

Another way to make the distinction is to say the power we are speaking of here is not political power but spiritual power and energy.

Here's a story from my experience that I hope says something about energy, the energy and power of God, in worship.

I recall one Sunday when the sermon ended with a particularly powerful story of God's graciousness and unpredictability, a story about the way God had acted in the life of a young man who described himself as "the teenager from hell." Despite the past that such a phrase suggests, this young man found himself, to his astonishment, called to ministry.

As the preacher turned from the pulpit "you could," as one of my parishioners sometimes said, "have heard a pin drop." What happened next was crucial. The scheduled hymn was "Amazing Grace." But no one "announced" the hymn or gave us silly instructions about where to find it in the hymnal (all that was already in the printed program). No one directed people to stand, as in "Let us now all stand to sing this wonderful hymn of faith."

After a few moments of silence a pianist simply began to play "Amazing Grace" softly. Without words the musician invited the congregation (who seemed by consensus to have decided to remain seated) to begin singing. We sang two verses accompanied, gently, by the piano. On the third verse, the pianist dropped out, so that we heard only our own voices in vulnerable harmony. The piano then rejoined us on the fourth and fifth verses. That third verse was aching and magical. After the hymn, and another brief silence, another worship leader stood and we were led into prayer, with the simplest of invitations, "Will you pray with me?"

Many things happened here that allowed the energy and the power of God to be active, present, and felt. But we, human beings, didn't make it happen. It is God's power, freely given, uncontrolled. We could have kept it from happening if the sermon had been too

---

15. Springer, *Nurturing Spiritual Depth*, 12.

Part Six: The Church of the Future

abstract or heady or the preacher not himself vulnerable and open, or if another worship leader had popped up right after the sermon to announce the hymn or direct people to the page and tell them to stand, or if the musician had chosen the organ rather than the piano and moved into a too loud, all-stops-out version of the hymn thus overwhelming the congregation's song, or if the pianist had insisted on playing an entire verse of the hymn as an introduction and doing so in a way indifferent to what had just happened.

But none of these things took place. The worship leaders and the congregation cooperated with the energy and allowed God to have God's way with us. And it was an experience of power, of God's power that empowered God's people for faithful living. When this power is present and active people are enlivened. They are put in touch with something that is truly renewing. And the people were healed and transformed.

You'll notice that in this illustration the paradox of "less is more" is at work. There's less chatter or chatting, no directions or explanations, more silence. A silence that was itself full. There are fewer words, but arguably more experience of the Word, the Logos of God.

The worship leaders were sensitive to the energy in the room, that spirit moving in the congregation. Rather than blocking it with unnecessary words or instructions, they helped to channel it. While this account is my own, you'll find a number of other examples and illustrations in Springer's work.

An awful lot of worship in the mainline Protestant tradition is pretty head-centered and, from the point of view of energy, anemic. Sadly, people sometimes leave worship with less energy—more depleted and overwhelmed—than when they came. Which is a recipe for church decline.

By criticizing "head-centered" I am not suggesting that our worship should be anti-intellectual or that sermons should lack careful thought. Quite the contrary. We are called to worship with our minds as well as our hearts, doing our best thinking and preparing.

I am, however, saying that frequently our worship only mirrors our predominant experience in modern, Western culture. That experience is heavily analytical, dominated by the left brain, and what you might call "judge-y." It's why people can do their shopping list while in church without noticing any real disconnect.

Here again, we are one might say in need of "recovery." We have overdosed, as it were, on the rational.

In her amazing poem, "Contraband," Denise Levertov gets at the way we have overdosed on reason.

> The tree of knowledge was the tree of reason.
> That's why the taste of it
> drove us from Eden. That fruit
> was meant to be dried and milled to a fine powder
> for use a pinch at a time, a condiment.
> God had probably planned to tell us later
> about this new pleasure.
> We stuffed our mouths full of it,
> gorged on but and if and how and again
> but, knowing no better.
> It's toxic in large quantities; fumes
> swirled in our heads and around us
> to form a dense cloud that hardened to steel,
> a wall between us and God, Who was Paradise.
> Not that God is unreasonable—but reason
> in such excess was tyranny
> and locked us into our own limits, a polished cell
> reflecting our own faces. God lives
> on the other side of that mirror,
> but through the slit where the barrier doesn't
> quite touch ground, manages still
> to squeeze in—as filtered light,
> splinters of fire, a strain of music heard
> then lost, then heard again.[16]

A good part of this recovery depends on worship leaders considering and paying attention to energy, in the sense Springer uses the term, in worship. Many of the best worship leaders do this

---

16. Levertov, *Evening Train*, 127. Used by permission.

Part Six: The Church of the Future

intuitively. But all of us can be helped by being more intentional about the energy, a category that shifts the focus of our attention in exactly the right ways as it makes God and God's power the focus of our worship.

Sending love . . .

Rethinking "Mission"

Dear Ones,

Recently I was talking with a friend who had just returned from a church mission trip to Guatemala, where he participated in a Habitat for Humanity house building project.

He said, "I received so much more than I gave." I said, "Wow, say more, what did you receive?"

He thought for a moment and said, "The people we worked with had so little, but they gave us so much love, love and joy. I was changed by that."

As you probably know, this is not an uncommon story. But it is often said with some degree of embarrassment, as if to say, "I was there to give, but really I was the one who received."

I've come to the conclusion that we shouldn't be embarrassed about this transformation of our expectations. Rather, we should find in it the reason for our ministries of service and justice.

Why do we do these things? Like build homes, serve meals, tutor children, visit those in prison? We may say, "To help the needy," or "to make the world a better place," or even, "Because Jesus said we should." There's nothing, of course, wrong with any of those answers.

But in the time after Christendom (Christian dominance of our culture) and in the new post-Christian future, a better reason for these ministries of service and justice may be that their purpose is to change the lives of our members.

Part Six: The Church of the Future

As I see it, the main task of the church in our new time is forming people in a particular faith and way of life, a life shaped by Jesus and following him.

Much of what churches have called "mission" or "social outreach" or "justice work" is a crucial way in which we change the lives of our own members, just as the man who had been on that mission trip in Guatemala found his life changed.

That's been true for me. From an early age, the church has changed my life by involving me in service, in sharing, and in interactions with people I would not have had if left to my own devices. I picketed a movie theater to protest segregation when I was just twelve. My church got me on those picket lines.

Another friend has gotten involved in church ministry at one of our state prisons. Twice a month he goes with others to the "Special Offender Unit," at the state prison where he spends an hour each in a visit with three different inmates. Speaking of that experience recently, he gestured toward his heart and said that he had discovered something as a result of these visitations, a "tender place" had been born in him for these men he visited.

As a pastor, I have encouraged people to reflect on their experiences of service and justice work by considering three questions: "What did I give?" "What did I receive?" "Where was God in this experience?"

I have also encouraged that we don't boil "mission" down to writing a check. Money is important, of course. But I've tried to encourage the idea that mission means more than sending money. It means sending ourselves.

The idea here was to make it a little more explicit that "mission" is a part of the overall faith formation and disciple-making work of the church.

Jesus said that in serving "the least" among us we are serving him. If that is true then we should not be surprised that in serving and sharing, we do also receive, and receive in ways that may change our own lives profoundly.

A colleague, Dan Hotchkiss, helped me think about "mission" in this somewhat new way. Dan wrote, "Congregations can and do make a difference to the lives of those they help through the outreach ministries they sponsor. But they make an even greater difference in the lives of their own members. In planning outreach ministries, it is important to remember that the lives we can transform most may be our own."[17]

The church of the future will be, I think, clear that we are more than another charitable institution or agency. We are in the business of changing lives. And as Dan writes, "The lives we can transform most may be our own."

All four of these letters in the "Church of Future" section ("Building the Front Porch," "Telling the Truth," "Pay Attention to the Energy," and this one, "Rethinking Mission") are predicated on the idea that there has been a sea change in North American culture in the last fifty years.

We no longer live in a nominally Christian, "churched" society. We live in a society that is in many respects "post-Christian" and "post-church." While many simply lament this (and at times I have also), I really see it as a wonderful, if challenging, opportunity. It is an opportunity to see everything we do as faith formation, as helping people to grow in faith and a way of life shaped by Christ's love and power.

And in this sense, every congregation is a "mission outpost" in the secular, materialistic, and pluralistic world of twenty-first-century America.

With this in mind, I see this as a good time to be a minister, a church leader. And hope you will find it to be that way also.

Sending love . . .

---

17. Hotchkiss, "What Is the Mission of Missions?"

Conclusion

Delight in Your Calling

I once heard a wise preacher say, "No excitement for the preacher, no excitement for the congregation." I'm totally sure that she wasn't saying, "Act excited, charged up, like a contestant on a TV quiz show." That is, she wasn't saying we are to feign or pretend excitement, not at all. I am saying, as I think she was, that doing the work that good preaching requires and hearing a word that grabs you by scruff of your neck so that you can't wait to share it generates excitement. If you're excited, chances are a lot better that the congregation will be true. The converse doesn't require stating.

Occasionally, we go to hear a live band or other artist, as I did last month at the O.K. Theater in the small town of Enterprise, Oregon. It was the CD release party for a young woman who had grown up there. The place was packed. And as the band came on stage and swung into action you could see and hear their delight, their joy, in what they were doing together. It radiated out, their delight becoming our own. There's something to be learned from such experiences.

So, in conclusion, delight in your ministry.

It is so easy to not do that. After your first time attending an ecumenical Bible study for preachers in your new area, you reported, Laura, that many of the clergy seemed pretty negative, complaining a lot about where they were or about their congregations. I understand that we all need to let off steam at times, and that people in the church can be frustrating as hell, but too many clergy let the burden of it overshadow the joy. To go back to my earlier letter on self-care, it is as if by looking totally worn out, exasperated, or discouraged we will certify our status as suffering martyrs of the faith and elicit sympathy. But "I'm suffering more than you" is really a sad game to play. And few are drawn to such neediness.

We are drawn to those who find reason and occasion to delight in the gospel, in the ministry, in the church, whether despite or because of its quirkiness and humanity. We are drawn most of all to those who delight in the strange ways and work of a living God, to the power that we can witness to but not control, to God's ways which are not, as Isaiah said, our ways.

Another caveat. I am not saying there aren't times for seriousness and an appropriate sense of gravity. Absolutely, there are. Moreover, I'd say worship is, as C. S. Lewis somewhere paradoxically described "joy," "the serious business of heaven." An overly casual or informal approach to worship suggests to me that there is not really much at stake here.

So, no, I'm not suggesting you must be always light and bubbly, never serious. Actually, I'm sort of sick of that. But I am suggesting that at some deep-down level you need to delight in what we've got going on here as church, as the people of this unexpected God.

What is the source of such delight? It has many possible sources. One is the people of the church themselves, who are, as stated, quirky, human, frustrating, and delightful. Another, I've mentioned time and again, is Scripture and how challenging and transformative it so often proves to be.

But one crucial source of our delight is Jesus. I couldn't have always said that. At times Jesus, or how Jesus was portrayed, I found more off-putting than delightful. In my encounters with more evangelical Christians I sometimes found them asking, "Do you love Jesus?" as if it were a test. Give the right answer and you're in. Failing that . . . outer darkness!

Not long ago, while reading Francis Spufford's marvelous book, *Unapologetic: Why, Despite Everything, Christianity Can Still*

CONCLUSION

Make Surprising Emotional Sense, I found myself enthralled by his chapter on Jesus, which is titled "*Yeshua.*" Of *Yeshua*, Spufford writes, "And he is never disgusted. He never says that anything—anyone—is too dirty to be touched. That anyone is too lost to be found. Even in situations where there seem to be no grounds for human hope, he will not agree that hope is gone beyond recall. Wreckage may be written into the logic of the world, but he will not agree that it is all there is. He says, more can be mended than you fear. Far more can be mended than you know."[18]

Reading Spufford, I realized he was describing the Jesus that I had come to know through the years, the Jesus I met in the New Testament and in risen One I had met in life. And I realized one other thing. I loved this Jesus.

In the end, our delight in him, in his table-turning, world-shattering, dying and rising way among us. You are one of his messengers. Delight in this calling.

Sending love . . .

---

18. Spufford, *Unapologetic,* 127.

Bibliography

Baskette, Molly Phinney. *Standing Naked Before God: The Art of Public Confession.* Cleveland: Pilgrim, 2015.
Bolz-Weber, Nadia. *Accidental Saints: Finding God in All the Wrong People.* New York: Convergent, 2015.
Bonhoeffer, Dietrich. *Life Together.* New York: Harper and Row, 1958.
Copenhaver, Martin, and Lillian Daniel. *This Odd and Wondrous Calling.* Grand Rapids: Eerdmans, 2014.
Friedman, Edwin H. *A Failure of Nerve: Leadership in the Age of the Quick Fix.* New York: Seabury, 2007.
Heifetz, Ronald, and Marty Linsky. *Leadership on the Line: Staying Alive Through the Dangers of Leading.* Cambridge, MA: Harvard Business Review Press, 2017.
Hoffman, Paul. *Faith Forming Faith.* Eugene, OR: Cascade, 2012.
———. *Faith Shaping Ministry.* Eugene, OR: Cascade, 2013.
Hotchkiss, Dan. "What is the Mission of Missions?" *Clergy Journal,* September 2006.
Levertov, Denise. *Evening Train.* New York: New Directions, 1990.
Peterson, Eugene. *Working the Angles: The Shape of Pastoral Integrity.* Grand Rapids: Eerdmans, 1987.
Placher, William C. *Unapologetic Theology: A Christian Voice in a Pluralistic Conversation.* Louisville: Westminster John Knox, 1989.
Robinson, Anthony B. *Transforming Congregational Culture.* Grand Rapids: Eerdmans, 2003.
———. *Stewardship for Vital Congregations.* Cleveland: Pilgrim, 2011.
Robinson, Anthony B., and Robert W. Wall. *Called to Lead: Paul's Letters to Timothy for a New Day.* Grand Rapids: Eerdmans, 2012.
Sloyan, Gerard. *Worshipful Preaching.* Minneapolis: Fortress, 1984.
Springer, Janice Jean. *Nurturing Spiritual Depth in Christian Worship: Ten Practice.* San Jose, CA: Resource, 2009.
Spufford, Francis. *Unapologetic: Why, Despite Everything, Christianity Can Still Make Surprising Emotional Sense.* New York: Harper One, 2012.

www.ingramcontent.com/pod-product-compliance
Lightning Source LLC
Chambersburg PA
CBHW020205090426
42734CB00008B/947